THE BRITISH HORSE SOCIETY

MANUAL OF EQUITATION

MANUAL OF
EQUITATION
The Complete Training of Horse and Rider

The Kenilworth Press Limited

First published in 1982, under
the title *Equitation*, by
Country Life Books in association with
the British Horse Society

This paperback edition published in 1992 by
Kenilworth Press Ltd
Addington
Buckingham MK18 2JR

in association with
The British Horse Society
The Deer Park
Stoneleigh
Kenilworth
Warwickshire
CV8 2XZ

© The British Horse Society, 1982, 1984, 1990, 1992
First edition 1982
Second edition 1984
Third edition 1990
Paperback edition 1992
Reprinted 1994, 1997, 1998

British Library Cataloguing in Publication Data
A catalogue record for this book is available from
the British Library

ISBN 1-872082-38-6

Typeset by Rapid Communication Ltd
Printed in Great Britain by
Hillman Printers (Frome) Ltd

Contents

Preface   7

Part 1 – Training the Rider

1   The Position of the Rider   11
2   Establishing the Basic Position
         on the Lunge   20
3   The Theory of the Aids   29
4   The Use of the Aids   37

Part 2 – Training the Horse

5   The Gaits   49
6   Lungeing   57
7   The Initial Training of the Horse   66
8   The Basic Training of the Horse   75
9   Advanced Training on the Flat   102
10   Training the Horse to Jump   112
11   Cross-country Training   122

Index   137

Preface

The British Horse Society's *Manual of Equitation* is based on the classical lines first written about by Xenophon (430-354 BC), maintained by the Spanish Riding School in Vienna and now amended for competitions by the Fédération Equestre Internationale.

Whilst it is difficult, if not impossible, to lay down hard and fast rules on the training of the horse and rider, and horsemastership in general, the *Manual of Equitation* is a concensus of opinion of the national authorities and represents the general view in Britain of equitation and horsemastership. No absolute doctrine has evolved, for Britain is a country where individuality is cherished and different horses, riders and trainers may be suited to different methods. Where, therefore, two methods are practised extensively and successfully in Britain, both are discussed.

This book is the result of many eminent members of the British Horse Society devoting a good deal of time voluntarily to discussing and writing about the subject.

The *Manual of Equitation* has been edited by Jane Kidd and Barbara Slane Fleming FBHS and illustrated by Eve Littleton and Patricia Frost.

PART 1

Training the Rider

1   The Position of the Rider

INTRODUCTION

The basis of all equitation is the ability of the rider to sit in the saddle in the correct classical position and to be able to maintain this position with minimum tension under all circumstances. The word 'classical' is not used in a pedantic way but refers to a position which has become classical because it has evolved through the ages as the most practical way of riding a horse. Xenophon (430 to 354 BC) wrote of it; it is taught by the Spanish Riding School; and, subject to the certain modifications adopted by the Fédération Equestre Internationale, FEI, it is the basis of this book.

The aim is that a rider should place as much of his weight as possible where the horse can most easily carry it: that is, just behind the withers, near to the animal's centre of balance (also its centre of gravity). By using an upright position the rider can remain in balance with the horse and this is essential if horse and rider are to work together in harmony. Any deviation from this ideal position will be reflected in the horse's way of going and/or his temperament. It is, therefore, essential that every serious horseman works to achieve a truly classical seat until such a position becomes instinctive to him.

The above applies also to the classical jumping position, which is achieved by closing the angles of hip, knee and ankle joints, while remaining in balance with the horse.

THE BASIC POSITION

The position described in detail in the following paragraphs is that to be adopted for riding on the flat. As well as being the one from which a rider can most easily influence his horse, it is also the most elegant. The rider sits square in the lowest part of the saddle, his weight equally distributed on his seat bones and absorbed by the seat, thighs and feet, the latter resting on the stirrups with only enough weight to keep the stirrups in place. The rider's point of balance is close to that of the horse: i.e. behind the horse's withers. There must be a minimum of tension, physical or mental, if the correct position is to be achieved and maintained. The muscles should have 'tone' – firmness which lies between extreme relaxation and tension.

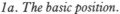

1a. The basic position.   *1b. Hollow back.*   *1c. Collapsed seat.*

OUTLINE FROM THE SIDE

Viewed from the side, the correct outline is shown in Fig. 1a, with a vertical line running through the rider's ear, shoulder, hip and heel. This line remains unchanged except in the rising trot. The position of the body viewed from the side should be:

• *Head.* The rider looks in the direction in which he is going, but if he needs to look down, he does so with the eyes only. The head should not be dropped nor poked forward, and the jaw should not be stiff.

• *Shoulders.* Should be down and well back without being stiff. This is achieved by expanding the chest rather than squaring the shoulders.

• *Back.* The body is upright, as in Fig. 2a, with the back straight but supple. It must not be hollowed or collapsed except to the extent that it follows the natural curvature of the spine.

• *Waist.* Should not be allowed to collapse backwards (collapsed seat), forwards (hollow seat), or to one side (collapsed hip.) (Fig. 2b.)

• *Hip joints.* These should be pressed slightly forward, with the pelvis upright so that the side seams of the breeches are upright and at right angles to the horse's back.

• *Legs.* The thighs should be flat on the saddle. The muscles should have minimal tone and tension in the thigh, hip joint, or anywhere in the leg. The knee points to the front, as does the toe, helping the rider to sit deeper in the saddle. The knee joint should not be forced into the saddle but should be relaxed so that the lower leg hangs down, lying softly on the horse's side. The legs should have the tone to maintain a constant contact with the horse's sides.

• *Feet.* The widest part of the foot rests on the stirrup iron with only sufficient weight to retain the irons. The stirrup irons should be level, with no extra weight on the inside or outside of the foot, the heel slightly lower than the toe with the ankle joint remaining supple.

• *Arms and hands.* The upper arm should be relaxed, hanging down and

12

2a. The rider's position viewed from the rear. Rider sitting upright.

2b. Collapsed right hip.

not behind the vertical. The shoulders and elbow joints should be flexible to allow the hands to follow the movements of the horse's head. There should be a minimum of tension in the forearm and in the hand and there should be a straight line from the elbow, through the hands to the horse's mouth. Looking from above, the straight line will run from the outside of the forearm, through the back of the hand, down the rein, to the horse's mouth. The thumb should be uppermost. The reins are held at the base of the fingers and come out over the top of the hand, where the thumb rests lightly on them. The fingers should be closed but not clenched, so that if the rider were holding a bird in each hand, the bird would be allowed to breathe but not to fly away.

OUTLINE FROM THE REAR

Viewed from the rear (Fig. 2a) a straight line would run through the middle of the rider's head, down the spine, through the centre of the back of the saddle and the horse's spine. On turns and circles the angle of the rider's body should stay exactly in line with the angle of the horse's body in relation to the ground: i.e., if the horse leans to the inside so must the rider.

• *Head*. The head and neck must be square on the shoulders and not tilted to either side.

• *Shoulders*. The shoulders should be at equal height without hunching or stiffness.

3a. *The position of horse and rider on a straight line.*   3b. *Turning to the right.*

● *Elbows.* The elbows should be level with one another, not stretched away from the body nor glued to the sides, and should hang naturally.

● *Seat.* The hip joints should be square to the front, with the weight resting evenly on both seat bones, the central seam of the breeches being in line with the centre of the saddle.

● *Lower legs.* The lower legs should be level with one another. They should hang down, not stretched from the horse's sides and with the inside of the lower legs quietly in contact with the horse's sides.

● *Feet.* The feet should be level, and should have equal weight on both stirrup irons without having more weight on the inside or outside of the irons. The ankles should be at equal angles.

THE SEAT

To use the seat correctly when riding it helps to understand its anatomy and methods of movement.

THE RELEVANT AREAS ARE:

The thighs: (femurs) which at their upper ends form the balls of the ball and sockets of the *hip joints*. The sockets of the right and left hip joints are about one third the way up the right and left *hip bones* (each hip bone consists of the ilium above, the ischium below and behind, and the pubis below and in front – Fig. 4.) The two hip bones form the front, sides and part of the back of the *pelvis* which is an oval-shaped (in horizontal section), almost rigid girdle. The lowest points of the pelvis are the *seat bones*. The ridges

14

of bone at the front of the pelvis which can be felt just below the waist are the *iliac crests*. The lower forward points of the pelvis which can be felt at the bottom of the abdomen are right and left *pubic bones*. At the back, the ring of the pelvic girdle is completed by the *sacrum*. This consists of fused rigid vertebrae which articulate with the *lumbar vertebrae* which run from just above to just below the waist. They are mobile, and above them the *thoracic vertebrae* are more rigid. On either side of the lumbar vertebrae are the *loins* which are the sections of the body on both sides of the spine lying between the hip bones and the false ribs. These are the ribs that are not attached to the breastbone.

THE RIDER CAN MOVE HIS SEAT BECAUSE:

☐ The lumbar spine is mobile.

☐ The pelvis can be tipped. From the pivot of where the rigid sacrum (rear section of the pelvis) and the mobile lumbar vertebrae are connected, the pelvis can be tipped forwards (iliac crests forward, pubic bones backward), and backwards, largely through use of the abdominal and back muscles.

☐ The hip joints enable the thighs and seat to move independently of each other.

THE PELVIS CAN ALSO BE:

☐ Tipped sideways (by bending the lumbar vertebrae) when one hip joint is lowered and moves sideways to result in a collapsed hip. (See page 13.)

☐ Turned so that in relation to the trunk this will result in one seat bone moving forward and round and the other backward in the opposite direction.

The hips. The term tends to be used loosely and may refer to the hip joints, or the hip bones, or the iliac crests, or the medical definition of the ischium, ilium and pubis. In this book, to avoid confusion the medical definition for the hips is used.

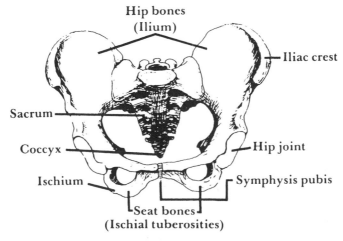

4. The pelvic girdle.

POSITION IN MOVEMENT ON THE FLAT

Walk. The horse walks in four time. He nods his head as each foreleg comes to the ground, and to keep the correct rein contact the rider's hands must invite this movement and not restrict it. The fingers remain closed on the reins and the correct contact is maintained. The rider remains sitting upright, but his supple seat moves to allow and not to restrict the horse's body movements. When the horse walks well there is considerable movement of his back muscles. This movement is essential if the horse is to remain supple, co-ordinated and free in his gaits. Therefore the rider must allow this movement to occur through supple action of his loins, but not his upper back. It is usual for the pelvis to move in the rhythm of the gait. A good exercise both for developing suppleness and feel is to allow the seat bones to move alternately so that as the left hind leg is lifted forward the rider allows his left seat bone forward in accordance with the horse's muscle movement and then the right seat bone with the right hind leg. This movement in the rider's seat and loins should not be exaggerated and should be barely perceptible to an onlooker.

Rising trot. The horse trots in two-time. The rider rises on one beat of the trot and sits on the next beat; it is essential that this is done in perfect balance so as not to upset the horse's rhythm. The rider's body is inclined slightly forward from the pelvis with the pelvis tipped forward, and he should sit softly without allowing the weight to go backwards. The shoulders and elbows allow the hands to go with the movement of the horse's head and neck, which in the trot hardly move.

Sitting trot. The rider does not rise but remains sitting, with his seat in contact with the saddle. The body remains upright. The movement of the horse's back is absorbed mostly through the rider's loins but also through the seat, thighs, knees and ankles. The hands keep consistent, elastic contact. The spring of the trot is such that in absorbing the movement, the rider should feel rather as though he is riding the crests of small waves. Thus, the thighs feel supple and the pelvis is cushioned by the seat. As in the walk, the rider's movement must not be exaggerated, resulting in the back hollowing or the waist collapsing. Any excess tenseness or gripping will cause the rider to bump instead of remaining in a quiet balanced position in contact with the saddle on the horse's back.

Canter. The horse canters in three-time. In the canter, the level of the horse's body alters from front to rear. The rider must therefore adjust to this alteration in the levelness of the horse as well as absorbing the up and down spring. The rider must absorb the bounding movement of the canter with his loins and seat and not by swinging his upper body backwards and forwards – which is a very common fault. The hip joints need to be pressed forward, the shoulders remaining on the vertical (not forward) and square to the horse's shoulders. The loins move to follow the undulating movement of the canter. The three hoof beats should be felt. The rider must retain a balanced seat, not slipping to one side of the saddle. Some riders press the hip joint corresponding to the leading leg slightly more forward than the other: i.e., if the near is leading, then the left seat bone should be forward. The rider's legs must remain long, with the inside leg beside the girth and the outside slightly further back. There must be no drawing up of either leg.

THE JUMPING POSITION

When jumping, or indeed when galloping on the flat, the rider must modify the basic seat, already described, partly to maintain his balance but also to take his weight off the horse's back.

TO ADOPT THE JUMPING POSITION, THE RIDER:

- ☐ Shortens his stirrup leathers (the length depending on the work to be carried out), which closes the angles of the hips-knees-ankles.
- ☐ Inclines his body forward from the pelvis, sliding the seat back a little (the seat may be kept in light contact with the saddle or not, as desired).
- ☐ Increases the weight on the thigh, knee and inside of the stirrup.
- ☐ Turns his toes slightly out so as to tighten the leg muscles.
- ☐ Remains looking forward and with his back flat.
- ☐ Holds his hands well in front of him, in a straight line from the elbow through the forearm, hands and rein to the mouth: although the elbows may leave the sides, as they move forward.

The result is that the rider's weight is taken off the horse's back and the rider is able to stay in balance when travelling at speed.

FAST WORK

In fast work on the flat the rider must take care that:

- ☐ The stirrups are short enough: otherwise the rider tends to stand in his stirrups and open the angle of the knee. The result is that the seat bones are not close enough to the saddle.
- ☐ The rider's body is not too far forward: i.e., the angle is not more than 45° from the vertical.
- ☐ The reins are shortened to ensure the rider's hands are well in front of the body.

THE POSITION IN MOVEMENT WHEN JUMPING (Fig. 5)

The jumping position described above is the one generally taught to riders. The position at the various stages of jumping a fence are:

5. Positions from the stride before take-off to the landing.

● *The approach.* The approach is made in the basic jumping position described above, making sure that the angle of the body is not more than approximately 45° in front of the vertical. The seat bones may be just clear of, brushing, or lowered into, the saddle. Care must be taken not to get in front of or behind the movement when riding the last stride, but to stay in balance. This is particularly important with young or green horses.

● *The take-off.* Depending on the size of the fence, the angle of the rider's body to the horse is closed, bringing the chest nearer to the mane. This must not be overdone nor must the angle of the knee be opened excessively. The knee must always be forward, pointed, and deep in the saddle. The rein contact is lightened and the hands follow the movement of the horse's head and neck. The lower leg should remain in the same position during this phase and throughout the jump.

● *In mid-air.* Over the top of the fence the rider maintains this position.

● *The descent.* On the descent the body remains inclined forward, and although the seat bones may brush the saddle, there should be no weight on them.

● *The landing.* The rider brings his body back to the original position with the stride after landing.

MODIFIED POSITION

Many riders use a modified jumping seat, adapted from that described on page 17. The difference between the two positions is one of degree, and experienced riders should be able to adapt their position between the two as necessary. The essential factor is to maintain a balanced scat.

In the modified position, the stirrup leathers are longer: the amount varying according to the rider's conformation and suppleness. The seat bones rest on the saddle but the main weight is borne by the inside of the thigh and knee.

The body is upright, or nearly upright, but not behind the vertical.

The hands are well in front of the rider, with the elbows slightly in front of the top of the hips (the iliac crests). There is a straight line from the elbow, through the forearm, hand and rein, to the mouth.

THE POSITION AT THE VARIOUS STAGES OF A JUMP ARE:

• *The approach.* The approach is made in the above position. The contact is kept the same throughout the approach.

• *The take-off.* The angle of the hip joint is closed, bringing the chest nearer to the horse's mane.

The weight is taken off the seat bones although the breeches may still brush the saddle, depending on the size of the fence.

The contact is lightened and the hands follow the movement of the horse's head and neck.

• *In mid-air.* Over the top of the fence the rider stays forward until the horse starts the descent.

• *The descent and landing.* The body on descent becomes more nearly upright and, on landing, resumes the approach position, the lower leg remaining in the correct position throughout.

A BALANCED SEAT

The two positions described are variations of a balanced seat. Either can be adopted according to the requirements of the horse and/or rider. The modified position enables the rider to control his horse's impulsion and stride better when coming into a fence and on landing. Horses who are lazy or likely to refuse may be more easily controlled from this position; but it requires considerably more agility on the rider's part if he is not to be left behind the movement with possible damage to the horse's back. It is usually advisable to 'ride in' in the basic position, especially on a young horse, as it takes the weight off the horse's back.

2   Establishing the Basic Position on the Lunge

INTRODUCTION

One of the best ways of establishing the correct position in the saddle and improving a rider's balance is for him to ride without stirrups both on and off the lunge. The main advantage of riding on the lunge is that the rider can leave the control of his horse to another, and can concentrate on his position, but he will only do this and ride without tension if he has complete confidence in the person doing the lungeing and if the horse is suitable.

This chapter is limited to giving guidance on how to establish a rider's basic position by riding on the lunge without stirrups. The technique of lungeing a horse without a rider differs considerably and is dealt with in Chapter 6, which also covers in more detail the facilities and tack required for lungeing.

There will come a time when the novice rider will wish to dispense with the lunge and to start riding, using reins and stirrups, and controlling his horse. This is acceptable once the rider has acquired a stable seat, and is the next step in his education. The means by which control is exercised are discussed in Chapters 3 and 4.

Even after the lunge has been dispensed with and the rider controls his own horse, riding without stirrups is still a most useful way of developing the correct position in the saddle. Many advanced riders do much work without stirrups, finding that they are more in harmony with their horse and so more effective.

RESPONSIBILITIES OF AN INSTRUCTOR

Instructing the rider. Anyone undertaking the lungeing of a rider should be well versed in lungeing and sufficiently knowledgeable to be able to correct the rider's position and help him to maintain it at all gaits. The instructor is responsible for modifying the horse's gaits and transitions to suit the rider. Sometimes he may use an assistant to lead the horse and give confidence to or support a novice in the first stages of riding on the lunge.

The rider's safety. When lungeing a rider, the instructor is entirely responsible for his safety and must do everything possible to avoid anything untoward happening which will reduce the rider's confidence. Only if a rider can work without tension will work on the lunge be of value. An instructor should pay attention to the following points, all of which have a bearing on the horse's and rider's safety:

☐ Lungeing should be carried out in a satisfactory environment. (See below.)
☐ Tack should be strong and well fitted.
☐ The lunge horse should be suitable.
☐ Lessons should not be too long and must contain rest periods.
☐ Instructor, rider and horse should be correctly turned out.

The instructor should always wear gloves when handling a lungeing rein, and should discard his spurs. The rider should wear breeches and boots or jodhpurs and must wear a hard hat.

FACILITIES NEEDED

The lungeing area. Lungeing should always be carried out in a reasonably quiet place so that neither the horse's nor the rider's attention is distracted and the instructor's commands can be clearly heard by both. The going must be good. The whole area should be level and, if possible, should be enclosed as this will greatly increase a novice rider's confidence and help the horse's concentration. It follows that an indoor riding school is often an ideal site for a lesson but it is certainly not essential.

An outdoor area always can be marked off by use of straw bales, poles and jump stands or the like.

Tack. The tack needed when lungeing a horse and rider consists of:
● *A snaffle bridle.* The reins can be twisted around under the neck and the throat strap put through one of the loops (Fig. 17, page 58), but it is safer to knot the reins on the horse's neck so that the rider can pick them up in an emergency.
● *A cavesson.* This is fitted over the bridle and buckled under the chin like a dropped noseband, or above the bit like cavesson noseband, with the lunge rein fastened to the central swivel ring on the noseband. The noseband and cheek strap must be tightened sufficiently to prevent them pulling round or rubbing the horse's outside eye.
● *A lunge rein.* About 10 metres (33 ft) long, made of linen webbing or nylon, with a large loop at one end and a swivel joint, attached to a buckle or spring clip, at the other.
● *Side-reins.* These are about 2 metres (6 ft) long and must be used with caution and only fastened to the bit after the pupil has mounted, and removed before he dismounts. They should run horizontally from the girth about half way up the horse's sides to mouth. (For the correct length see page

62.) When not in use they should be clipped to the Ds of the saddle.

● *A saddle.* It is important for the saddle to fit both horse and rider. The use of a numnah is recommended.

● *A lunge whip.*

● *Brushing boots* for all four legs.

The lunge horse. Ideally, the horse to be used by a rider on the lunge should be a specialist at the job, but a lunge horse must do other work if he is not to become thoroughly stale. Temperament is very important and he must be obedient to the human voice – since, on the lunge, this will be the principle aid. The gaits should be comfortable. Circling is a strain on a horse and a fit and mature animal of six or over should be used. The time spent on the lunge should not exceed twenty minutes (excluding rest periods) if the horse is being used actively.

TECHNIQUE FOR LUNGEING A RIDER

The instructor. The instructor stands in the centre of the lungeing circle, which is normally about 15 metres (50 ft), or slightly less, in size and drives the horse round him, holding the lunge rein in the hand towards which the horse is moving, and holding the whip in his other hand. Instructors can hold the loop at the end of the lunge rein in either hand. The instructor must concentrate on the rider and on the horse's hind quarters rather than on his forehand. It is important to ensure that the horse describes a true circle, and the instructor should stand on one spot. A trained lunge horse should be obedient to the instructor's voice. The lunge whip should seldom have to be used, but when it is needed the horse should be lightly touched and usually above the hind fetlocks. Whenever the instructor moves closer to the horse, the whip should be reversed, with the thong trailing to the rear.

Length of a lungeing lesson. As already mentioned, a horse being used actively should not be lunged for more than some twenty minutes, excluding rest periods. Frequent rest periods will be needed, since riding without stirrups can be tiring for riders. The horse should be worked equally on each rein.

Preliminary work. Before the start of a lesson, an instructor will often wish to begin by lungeing the horse without a rider, to settle him down. Many riders like to 'warm up' by riding on the lunge but using their stirrups. Both measures may be used with advantage.

Adopting the correct position. The person lungeing and instructing must ensure that the rider takes up and maintains the correct position in the saddle as defined in Chapter 1. The rider, with the horse stationary, places himself in the deepest part of the saddle, with his weight on his seat bones and his legs hanging loosely down against the saddle. To achieve this position, he should take hold of the front of his saddle with both hands and gently pull his seat into the lowest part, making himself as upright as possible, so that a vertical line running from his ear through the point of his shoulder bisects his hip joint and touches the back of the heel. The side reins should not be attached until work on the move begins. The following two points should be particularly noted:

☐ There should be no deviation from the line, ear-shoulder-hip joint, although later the heel can come forward of this line without ill effect in the riding of horses. A rider sitting on his fork will tend to be in front of the vertical line and if he transfers his weight from his seat bones to his buttocks the tendency will be for him to be behind this line. (See Fig.1)

☐ The inner thigh muscles must be relaxed so that the knee lies sufficiently low on the saddle to adopt the correct position.

To assist in achieving the correct position. The following simple and short exercise may be carried out before starting work, either when halted or at a walk. The movements should never be jerky and the timing must be left to the rider, the exercise being repeated two or three times.

The rider, holding the front of the saddle, stretches both legs sideways away from the horse's side. He then allows the legs to relax completely and to fall gently back on to the saddle, the knee being as low as possible, without straining.

To build up confidence. At all three gaits and on both reins the rider can take one hand off the saddle and allow his arm to hang down just behind his thigh for a circle or two. The whole arm should be relaxed, as this exercise should begin to instil in the rider the importance of a relaxed upper arm once he is holding the reins. When he can let go of the saddle, both arms may be dropped together, care being taken that the waist does not collapse or the shoulders become rounded.

Work at the walk. Lungeing the rider at the walk can be used to give confidence to beginners or nervous riders. There is very little upward thrust in the movement of the horse's back, but an active walk will displace the rider's balance on a horizontal and slightly diagonal plane and riders must be taught that this motion must be absorbed through the suppleness of their loins and seat and must not result in a rocking action of the upper body.

Although all exercises that follow can be carried out at the walk, for more experienced riders the walk is best used for checking the rider's position and during rest periods when the rider is allowed to sit at ease.

Sitting to the trot. Once in the correct position at the walk and with the rider still holding the saddle if required, the horse can be sent quietly forward into a trot, as long as the speed, action and spring of it is well within the rider's capabilities. Advanced riders will instinctively try to influence this. They should normally not do so, but should accept what the horse offers and should concentrate on maintaining their own position with tone but without gripping. Only when the seat and balance are fully established should the seat be used to control the movement and action of the horse. At the sitting trot, the rider should adjust to the two-time rhythm of the trot and, remaining supple and with tone, allow the weight of the straight body to sink softly down into the saddle as each pair of diagonal legs meet the ground; horse and rider will then rebound as one during the periods of suspension. Once the rider has achieved this, he will be able to sit still in relation to the movement of his horse.

Rising to the trot. Rising to the trot without stirrups has little to commend it, except as a strengthening exercise for jumping and racing. Should a rider need to improve his technique, the stirrups should therefore be re-attached and the leathers so adjusted that he can make and easily retain contact, with the widest part of his foot on the iron and with the heel lower than the toe. It is important to adapt the length of leather to suit the rider's position and not the other way round. If the leathers are too short, either tension will develop – especially in the knees and ankles – or, more likely, the rider will move his seat back in the saddle. If too long, the rider will constantly be dropping his toes to make contact with the irons, so weakening his whole position.

Once the stirrups are the correct length and the horse is moving in a soft, springy trot the rider should allow this action gently to lift his seat bones from the saddle on every diagonal stride. To compensate for this movement the body should also go slightly forward from the top of the hip bones. Retaining this position the rider then sinks softly back into the saddle on the next stride. The feeling should be of 'going forward and down and not up in the air and back' (de Nemethy). The whole movement should be initiated by the action of the horse and not by the rider.

Changing the diagonal. When rising to the trot on the lunge the rider should rise in time with and as the horse's outside shoulder goes forward, thus returning to the saddle as that leg and the inside hind leg hit the ground. This is known as rising on, or using, the outside diagonal, which not only makes it easier for the horse to maintain his balance on the circle but also prevents one-sided muscular development. It also has an important part to play in the use of the aids once the horse is off the lunge. Riders should be encouraged constantly to change the diagonal by sitting down for one additional stride before rising again until they can tell instinctively which diagonal they are using.

Work at the canter. The difficulties entailed when riding at a canter on the lunge are greater than at the walk or trot and this should never be attempted without an experienced person in charge and in a quiet place away from other horses.

Centrifugal force is more noticeable at the canter, and riders should guard against the use of grip to maintain their position. The upper body should not rock in rhythm with the changing horizontal levels of the horse's back; this should be absorbed through supple loins and seat. Not all exercises can be carried out at the canter, and the suitable ones are mentioned in the following paragraphs.

EXERCISES

General. When a rider has the confidence and ability to let go of the saddle and to ride easily while maintaining his correct position without gripping, for about five minutes on each rein, further mounted exercises should be attempted. These are designed to improve the rider's position, suppleness and balance and, in the case of the novice, to increase his confidence.

The following general points apply to all exercises on the lunge whether at the walk, trot or canter, and should be observed by the rider and the person lungeing him or supervising the exercise:
□ As the basis of riding is rhythm, all exercises should be carried out rhythmically in time with the horse.
□ The exercises should develop balance, suppleness and strength without producing tension anywhere.
□ The movement of one part of the body should not be reflected in another part.
□ Breathing should be deep and controlled with a slight emphasis on exhalation, as this helps relaxation. No exercise in the saddle should make the pupil out of breath.
□ All exercises should be carried out on both reins. Few riders sit in an identical position on each side and most have a tendency to twist in the saddle, causing one leg to move forward and the other slightly back.
□ Twenty minutes excluding rest periods should be the maximum for work on the lunge for any but the most experienced riders.

The following exercises are suitable for riders on the lunge:
● *Correcting the position.* The rider holds the front of his saddle, keeps his seat firmly in the saddle as he straightens his body upwards at the same time as pulling gently down into the saddle and stretching down with both legs, i.e., there should be an upward and downward correction. This should be done immediately prior to transitions and is a useful exercise at other times. Later the muscle influence of these movements is used to warn the horse that something is about to be asked of him and to ensure the rider is in the correct position to apply the aids. The rider should develop the

25

habit of correcting his position prior to asking anything of the horse.

As the rider progresses, the same exercise may be carried out with the hands in the rein position: i.e., holding imaginary reins, great care being taken that the correct position is not lost, particularly during transitions.

• *Shoulder exercise.* In shoulder-shrugging the object is to remove any tension from the shoulders and the base of the neck. Both shoulders are drawn up as high as possible towards the ears (taking care not to tilt the head back or stick the elbows out), and then allowed to drop back into place. They must not be lowered hesitantly or be pulled down forcibly. This should be repeated five or six times; it must be done in an easy rhythm and without setting up any tension in the back or arms.

• *Head and neck exercises.* The object is to rid the neck and jaw of tension. These exercises are a logical follow-on to the previous one.

1. The head is allowed to turn steadily anti-clockwise and then clockwise. Care should be taken that the head does not tilt.

2. Without raising the chin, the head is rolled steadily first to one side and then the other, with the ear as nearly as possible resting on the shoulders, which must not be allowed to lift.

3. The head is allowed to roll steadily forward until the chin is resting on the chest. Care should be taken that the back does not become rounded.

N.B. 1 and 3 should be performed at the halt only.

• *Arm and shoulder exercises.* The object is to flatten and stretch the muscles of the abdomen and free the shoulder joints.

1. Steadily raise alternate arms with fingers stretched and the elbow joint straight until it reaches maximum height with the elbow joint beside the ear, palm facing forward.

2. Circle the arms slowly to the rear three or four times before returning to normal position. The exercise may then be carried out with both arms simultaneously. The swing should always be backwards and in rhythm with the horse's stride. No force should be used or effort made to complete a full backward circle.

3. Instead of circling the arms backwards, they may be moved backwards as far as they will go without strain, keeping the arm and fingers straight. The arm is then returned to the vertical position. In both 2 and 3 the shoulder and hip joints must remain parallel.

4. Raise the arms so that they are horizontal. Turn the body from the waist alternatively to the left and the right, while maintaining the arms on the horizontal and at 180° to each other. The seat must remain still. This can be done at the walk and trot.

• *Spine and hip joints.* The object of these exercises is to make the spine and hip joints supple.

1. ARM TURNING. Allow the arms to hang limply down and place one hand on the horse's withers and the other over the back of the saddle. Change position by twisting from the waist without losing correct position or the rhythm of the gait. The seat must not move in the saddle nor

the backward arm be taken beyond the line of the horse's spine. This exercise may be safely carried out at the halt, walk or trot, but the pupil should be fairly competent before attempting it at the canter.

2. JOCKEY POSITION. While holding the front of the saddle, draw the legs up, closing the angles of the ankles, knees and hips, and come forward with the body into the racing position. At first, maintain the position for a few strides but gradually hold for longer and longer. This can be done at the walk and trot.

3. SCISSORS. Lengthen legs and while maintaining seat bones in the saddle swing alternately one leg back and the other forwards. This can be done at the walk and trot.

4. TOUCHING TOES. Take one hand and touch the toe on the opposite side. Repeat with other hand. This can be done at all paces.

• *Ankle exercise.* Turn ankles in as full a circle as possible, firstly clockwise and then anti-clockwise. This can be done at all paces.

The value of lungeing

☐ It is one of the best ways of establishing the correct position, which is important for three reasons: firstly, to balance the load that the horse is asked to carry; secondly, to enable the rider to apply the aids quietly and effectively; and, thirdly, to enable the rider to look as elegant as possible.

☐ It helps to make the rider supple and therefore more able to follow the movements of the horse.

☐ It helps the rider to learn how to 'feel', to analyse, and to allow and affect the horse's movement.

FITNESS OF THE RIDER

Every rider must be reasonably fit if he is to be able to maintain the correct position in the saddle, to assist his horse and to enjoy his riding. It is a surprising fact that the energy consumed in riding is of the same order as that used in such obviously physically demanding sports as running or cycling, so that even a novice requires a degree of basic fitness. For the advanced and the competitive rider, such as the jockey, three-day eventer, show jumper or dressage rider, a much higher standard of physical fitness is needed.

Methods of achieving fitness. While daily riding is in itself a good way of keeping fit, it is certainly not enough to reach the standard of fitness required for competition. For this, the rider's heart and lungs must work efficiently, and the muscles of the back and leg should be in particularly good condition. He or she must be supple in body, and excess fat must be avoided.

It is generally agreed that the best way to keep fit is to run regularly, although skipping, swimming and cycling are all useful aids to fitness. There are also many more mounted exercises suitable for riders of all stages; dismounted exercises and yoga, which help as well as promote suppleness and co-ordination. Many riders have found a study of the Alexander Technique extremely helpful in improving their riding abilities.

It is most important not to overdo physical training, which should always be progressive and should take into account the rider's age and medical condition. In special cases, medical advice should be sought before a strenuous course of training is undertaken.

3 The Theory of the Aids

INTRODUCTION

Aids are the language of horsemanship and, like all languages, have a basic structure, but it is emphasis and timing which lend them expression and refinement.

It is essential that anyone who wishes to ride well should understand the use, the reasons for, and the effect of the aids, before he tries to teach them to his horse. The horse must be taught stage by stage and with complete clarity until the rapport between rider and horse is built up to such a level that it appears that the rider has but to think for the horse to obey willingly. This is the essence of true horsemanship. A trainer who can combine intelligence with mental and physical control and co-ordination can produce a highly trained, alert and happy horse, working with ease and with complete confidence in his rider.

DEFINITION AND TYPES OF AIDS

An aid is the signal or means by which a rider conveys his wishes to his horse. It refers to any action by the rider which results in physical or mental communication between him and his horse.

Aids are sub-divided into natural and artificial as follows:
- *Natural aids.* The rider's voice, legs, seat and hands.
- *Artificial aids.* Whips, spurs and any form of strap (other than the reins) which control or position the horse, with or without the rider's help. Examples are standing or running martingales, draw or running reins. Only the whip and spur have a place in classical equitation and are the only artificial aids considered in this chapter.

THE VOICE

The voice by its tone can encourage, correct, soothe or reward. It is also used to give commands, particularly on the lunge and with a young horse when it is first ridden. The horse learns that sharp, quick commands 'walk on', 'trot', 'canter' mean to go forward, and low and drawn-out 'whoaa', 'wa-alk', 'ter-rot' to reduce the pace.

THE LEGS, SEAT AND HANDS

Although they are discussed separately below, the legs, seat and hands are always used in conjunction with one another as explained in the next chapter.

THE LEGS

The major functions are:
- ☐ To create forward movement.
- ☐ To activate the hind quarters.
- ☐ To indicate direction and to control the position of the horse.
- ☐ To move the horse laterally (sideways).

Identical use of the legs. The effect of using both legs by the girth is to encourage the horse to move forward. When first handled, any horse will react to human contact by withdrawing from it. As flight is his natural defence, when first mounted and feeling the legs of the rider enclosing his rib cage, the reaction is to move forward away from the pressure. This is the basis of all training and is developed and refined by constant repetition, until the slightest pressure with the inside of the rider's leg will result in the horse moving forward.

Individual use of the legs. Once this reaction of moving forward is established, the application of either of the rider's legs by the girth will encourage the horse to move the hind leg forward on that side. Since it will also be instinctive for the horse to try to evade the pressure on the ribs it will also tend to bring the leg forward and slightly under the weight of the body preparatory to turning the hind quarters away from the point of stimulus. This effect is used to move the horse laterally, but if it is not desired, and the horse is required simply to turn a corner, then the rider prevents the hind quarters falling out by placing his other leg slightly further back from the girth. Hence, while both legs cause the horse to go forward, the rider's inside leg by the girth accentuates the forward movement while the outside leg, slightly behind the girth, controls the hind quarters.

Response to the leg aids. The lower legs must always remain in quiet soft contact with the horse's sides. When a particular signal is required, the legs are used with a vibrant changing pressure and not a constant squeeze. They should be applied as lightly as possible and only when required, as repeated heavy thumping with the legs, heels or spurs will cause the horse to become dead to the leg.

N.B. A horse which reacts to leg aids by drawing back is said to be 'behind the leg', and a horse that goes freely forward at the slightest indication from the rider's legs is said to be 'in front of the leg'.

THE SEAT, INCLUDING THE WEIGHT

The major influences are on:
□ Impulsion.
□ Outline.
□ Direction.

Use of seat and weight aids. The seat aids can be used beneficially only if the rider can sit correctly, softly and quietly with the weight equally on both seat bones. He must allow the horse to remain supple and to swing his back. The novice rider should concentrate on using his seat only insofar as he allows the horse's movement to go 'through': i.e., he allows the horse's back muscles to operate freely so that the actions of the hind quarters and forehand are co-ordinated and not separated by a stiff back. Thus the rider should not sit heavily and stiffly, which would suppress the movement 'through' the horse's back and make the outline hollow. A rider can start to use the seat aids when he can feel the actions of the hind legs and his seat is independent enough to be able to apply an aid without setting up undesired changes or movements elsewhere in his body.

THESE AIDS CAN BE USED IN THE FOLLOWING WAYS:
□ To lighten the weight on the seat bones and allow the horse's back to come up.
□ To allow the horse's back muscles to swing by sitting passively with supple hips.
□ To request the desired rhythm.
□ In conjunction with the back and lower leg to engage the hind quarters and bring the hind legs more underneath.

On the young horse the weight must be used with great care: if it is not, the horse will hollow and tighten his back. This is why on a young horse most of the trot work is done rising and much of the canter work with the rider leaning slightly forward and off the horse's back. This is particularly important with Thoroughbreds. On the more trained horse, going in a correct round outline, the weight and the use of the back become very important aids.

On straight lines the rider's weight must be absolutely central.

On turns, circles, lateral work and in canter the weight is brought slightly to the inside by turning the body in the direction of the movement and putting more weight into the inside stirrup.

THE HANDS

The major influences are to:
□ Contain the impulsion created by the rider's legs and seat. (Impulsion is the energy created by the activity of the hind quarters.)

☐ Control the speed.
☐ Help the balance.
☐ Indicate direction.
☐ Control the bend and aid maintenance of outline.

The hands are only supplementary and complementary to the seat and leg aids. Except for the very young horse the rider should apply the leg (and seat) aids before the hands, otherwise the hind quarters will tend to fall out behind and the impulsion will be lost rather than contained.

Response to hand aids. Through the reins and the bit the hands are a telephone to the horse's brain and their use has a paramount effect on his mental and physical attitude. To be most effective the hands should:

☐ Never pull backwards.
☐ Remain still in relation to the movement of the horse and entirely independent of the action of any other part of the rider's body.
☐ Maintain a consistent light sympathetic but elastic contact with the bit (except when riding on a loose rein). The horse loses his sense of security if the rein contact is inconsistent.
☐ Keep the same weight in walk, trot and canter, taking care not to make the contact stronger in the faster gaits.

Individual use of the hands. The tension in the reins may not be the same in both hands when working on turns or circles, at the canter, and when correcting the natural crookedness of the horse. It is when working a straight horse on straight lines at the walk and trot that the rider should have an even feel in both hands. For most of the time the reins should be used as follows:

• *Outside hand.* The hand on the opposite side to the rider's inside leg will receive some of the impulsion sent forward from the horse's inside hind leg. To control this the rider maintains a positive contact with the horse, i.e. one that neither releases nor pulls back the rein but maintains a consistent sympathetic contact in relation to the movement and therefore goes with it.

• *Inside hand.* The inside hand accepts and guides the inside bend of the horse, a bend which is created by the rider's seat and leg aids. The contact should be light and flexible to encourage the relaxation of the horse's lower jaw and the acceptance of the bit.

The principle is that the outside hand maintains a positive contact which controls the pace and assists the balance, while the inside hand is more flexible and indicates the bend.

Riding on a long and on a loose rein. A horse can be ridden on a long rein, but the rider should maintain impulsion with his legs and seat while allowing the horse to relax and to stretch forward and down with his head and neck and to lengthen his stride. The rider, by opening his fingers, lets the reins slide as the horse asks for the extra length but does not completely lose contact. This is often described as keeping contact 'by the weight of the reins alone'.

There are times when a horse is ridden on a loose rein without any contact at all. A free walk, or walk on a loose rein, is ridden in the same way as a walk on a long rein, but all contact with the horse's mouth is abandoned and the horse is kept straight by the use of the rider's seat and legs alone.

Work on a long and loose rein may be used at all three gaits, providing impulsion and balance are maintained.

Methods of holding the reins. There are many different but acceptable methods of holding the reins. Some of the main ones are mentioned and illustrated in Figs 6 and 7.

In most methods of holding the reins, the reins run from the horse's mouth, through the fingers, across the palm of the hand and out between the thumb and forefinger, with the thumb on top of the rein. The hand must be lightly closed. In all cases it is the pressure of the thumbs on the reins over the forefingers which prevents the reins from slipping, and not the grip of a clenched hand or fingers.

• *Snaffle bridle.* When held in both hands, the reins pass between the third and fourth fingers, across the palm of the hand and out between the first finger and thumb; alternatively, the reins go round the outside of the little finger and out between the first finger and the thumb. When held in one hand, the most commonly used methods are to put the rein being moved between the thumb and first finger and out at the bottom of the hand, or to put it between the second or third finger and out between the first finger and thumb.

6a. *Snaffle reins held in both hands.*   6b. *Snaffle reins held in one hand.*

• *Double bridle.* When held in both hands, three recommended methods are:

   1. The bridoon rein passes outside the little finger, and the curb, or bit rein, between the third and little finger. Both reins then cross the palm of the hand and go out between the first finger and thumb. This is the most usual way of holding the reins of a double bridle.

7a. Double reins in both hands.   *7b. Double reins held in one hand.*

2. As in 1 above, except that the position of the bridoon and bit reins are reversed.

3. Both bit reins are held in one hand, separated by the second or third finger. The bridoon rein, on that side, passes outside the little finger. All three reins pass out between the first finger and thumb. The other bridoon rein is held between the fingers of the other hand.

The bit reins are adjusted to the required length on taking them up between the fingers, and thereafter are not altered, the horse being ridden on the bridoon reins in each hand.

Should the rider wish to hold the reins in one hand: e.g. the left hand, he has only to transfer the right snaffle rein to the left hand, placing it over the top of the index finger and allowing the slack to hang down from the palm.

THE ARTIFICIAL AIDS

The whip. The whip helps to reinforce the leg aids should they prove insufficient.

APPLICATION

It should be used quickly and lightly behind the leg to emphasise the aid or to ask for more attention.

On occasion it will be necessary to change the hand in which the whip is held. To do this all the reins are put into the hand holding the whip and the free hand then takes hold of the whip below the holding hand, the back of the hand towards the rider's body. The whip is brought quietly across to the other side with the tapered end of the whip passing in front of the rider's face; the rein is then retaken by the whip hand. An alternative method is to put all the reins into the hand holding the whip; then the free hand takes hold of the whip above the holding hand, and draws it through the hand. The whip is then brought quietly across to the other side, tapered and downwards. The reins are then picked up again.

34

The schooling whip is used for schooling on the flat. It should be between 0.90 metres (3 ft) and 1.2 metres (4 ft) so that it is long enough to apply without taking the hand off the rein. The wrist is flicked to result in a tickle or a tap whenever required, behind the rider's leg.

The shorter whip, used for jumping, must not exceed 75 cms (30 ins). The whip hand should be taken off the rein, and both reins should be held in one hand and the whip applied behind the leg. The rider should practise this action and the ability to change whip hands.

The spurs. Like the whip the spurs help to reinforce the leg aids should they prove insufficient. They should allow more unobtrusive aids to be given.

APPLICATION

When used, the spurs should only brush the skin. Spurs are a refinement of the aids and should not be used as a sole means of creating impulsion. The rider must be able to apply his legs without the spurs touching the horse.

Spurs are rarely used in the early training of a horse and are not suitable for use by inexpert horsemen.

The artificial aids are only brought into action if the legs are not effective.

SUMMARY

- ☐ The aim is for the aids to encourage the horse to go forward, straight and with rhythm.
- ☐ Ride from the inside leg into the outside rein.
- ☐ Use inside leg for impulsion, close to girth.
- ☐ Use outside leg for controlling quarters, a little back.
- ☐ Use inside rein for direction and bend.
- ☐ Use outside rein for balance, controlling pace and bend.
- ☐ Keep weight to inside in turns, circles and lateral work.
- ☐ Turn body in direction of movement.
- ☐ Always keep body upright.

Good aids are those which:
- ☐ Ensure that the forward impetus of the horse is given willingly and completely into the rider's control.
- ☐ Dictate the pace and/or the direction of the movement.
- ☐ Are unobtrusive.

Aids are misused if they:
- ☐ Position or restrain the horse's body or speed by force.
- ☐ Create more impulsion than the rider can control.
- ☐ Fail to create the impulsion needed to help the horse to accept the bit.
- ☐ Fail to allow the rider's weight to move in harmony with that of the horse.
- ☐ Fail to allow the hands to follow the horse's movement.

- ☐ Are neither definite nor clear enough for the horse to comprehend their meaning.
- ☐ Are used continually, even involuntarily and without reason or anticipation.
- ☐ Are used roughly, obviously, or to punish without justification.

4 The Use of the Aids

INTRODUCTION

This chapter describes how the rider uses the aids to convey his wishes to his horse. The aids are comparatively few but the way in which they are applied – for example, the degree of pressure of each leg and of contact in each rein – can vary greatly, and their use calls for skill and tact on the part of the rider.

For the aids to be most effective the rider must be in balance himself, and this is best achieved by establishing the correct position.

Definitions. For fuller definitions of the movements, refer to the British Horse Society's *Rules for Dressage*, and the Fédération Equestre Internationale (FEI) *Rules for Dressage Events*.

The terms '*inside*' and '*outside*' are used frequently and refer to the slight curve throughout the length of the horse's body, 'inside' always being the concave side of the horse when correctly bent, and vice versa; they do not refer to the sides of the school or manège.

FORWARD MOVEMENT

In all forward movement it is essential for the rider to look ahead at the point towards which he is asking the horse to move.

The first aid used by the rider is to activate the horse's hind legs into forward movement. To achieve this into the walk or trot (often referred to as 'moving off' or 'going forward into'); or into the canter (usually called 'striking off'), or for other upward transitions, the aids are as follows:

Moving off and upward transitions
The rider:
□ Checks his position.
□ Maintains a light contact through the reins with the horse's mouth.
□ Applies extra pressure with both legs by the girth – not a steady squeeze but a series of quick, vibrant touches with the inside of his calf muscles.
□ Advanced riders, who are able to feel the natural inclination of their horse to favour a left or right bend, may compensate for this when moving off into a faster gait by adopting the opposite position: i.e., position right on a

horse with a preference for a left bend. (See *Position right and left*, page 40.) This helps to maintain suppleness and keeps the horse straight.

Striking off into canter

The rider:

☐ Checks his position.

☐ Asks his horse for position right or left according to which leading leg is required. (See page 40.)

☐ Applies the outside leg back behind the girth to encourage the horse's hind leg on that side to move forward and so to start the sequence of the canter gait (page 51).

☐ Applies the inside leg by the girth to encourage forward movement.

☐ Moves the inside seat bone forward, and when the canter is established the weight comes slightly to that inner side.

☐ Moves the weight a little to the inside.

☐ Takes care to keep the horse straight and not allow the quarters to move to the inside.

Upward transitions within a pace

For transitions from collected to working, medium or extended gaits, the rider:

☐ Checks his position.

☐ Makes a half-halt to get the horse's hind legs more engaged.

☐ Applies his legs by the girth to lengthen the stride.

☐ With the reins, while containing the impulsion, allows the horse to lengthen his outline.

☐ Maintains a supple seat, through movement of his loins and hip joints, thus allowing the horse to swing his back.

NB: At the trot, during training, it is often advisable to rise.

CONTROLLING THE FORWARD MOVEMENT

The reins are used to control the forward movement, but except in the case of a very young horse their action must be in conjunction with the legs and seat aids in order to keep the hind quarters engaged. These rein aids are applied through sympathetic movement of the fingers and the hands.

Downward transitions

The rider:

☐ Checks his position.

☐ Makes several half-halts with the outside rein or with both reins, the former is more usual.

☐ Uses the legs and seat to engage the hind legs and lower the quarters so that the horse's forehand is lightened.

□ Uses the reins as little as necessary with a restraining but not restrictive movement. The slowing-down aid is usually given with the outside rein.

□ As soon as the new gait is established, rides forward by the use of the seat and legs ensuring that the rhythm of that new gait is maintained.

□ Takes care that his balance is maintained so that he is not left forward of the movement.

The half-halt (page 87). This is a hardly visible moderated version of the halt – 'the momentary collection of a horse in motion' (Von Blixen-Finecke).

The rider:

□ Applies momentarily the driving aids of the seat and the legs.

□ Restrains momentarily with his hands the horse's consequent desire to go forward so that the horse becomes more collected, rather than going faster.

□ Releases momentarily the pressure on the reins before restoring the original contact.

The halt (pages 87 and 94). The aids are the same as for all downward transitions, but in this case the restraining but allowing hands finally stop the movement. Even in the halt impulsion should not be allowed to escape, so the horse maintains a light contact with the bit and the rider's legs remain on the horse's side.

The rein-back (page 94)

The rider:

□ Establishes a square halt and takes care that the horse remains on the bit.

□ Eases the weight in the saddle by putting more weight into the stirrups and on the thighs.

□ Applies the legs just behind the girth.

□ Prevents the consequent inclination to move forward by restraining aids on the reins.

□ Releases the pressure on the reins as soon as the horse steps back. It is vital that the rider does not pull backwards on the reins as the horse will then resist or run back stiffly. The horse must also be kept straight by appropriate use of the rider's legs and, if necessary, the reins.

TURNS AND CIRCLES (Fig. 3, page 14)

In turns and circles the horse remains bent around the rider's leg. His hind legs should follow exactly in the track of the front legs. This is achieved by riding from the inside leg into the outside rein.

To turn or circle

The rider:

☐ Checks his position.

☐ Applies his fingers on the inside rein intermittently, to establish a more flexible contact and a slight bend, and thus indicate direction.

☐ Turns his body to the inside and transfers slightly more weight into the inside stirrup.

☐ Uses the outside rein to allow the bend of the horse's head and neck with a constant contact, unless he brings it into use to control the impulsion and the extent of the bend.

☐ Uses both legs and a supple seat to maintain impulsion, but the inside leg by the girth dominates and must be sufficiently effective to induce the horse to bring his hind leg, on that side, forward and slightly under the centre of his body; only then will the horse be able to follow the true line of the circle.

☐ Rests his outside leg slightly back. The leg remains in this position ready for use if the horse's hind quarters start to swing to the outside of the circle.

☐ Is very careful not to increase the weight of the inside rein.

Position right and left. A rider is said to be in position right when he has his right leg close to the girth, and his left leg a little behind the girth, therefore indicating a slight bend with the right rein and controlling the impulsion, speed and bend with the left rein. He is then said to be riding from the inside leg into the outside rein. In position left the aids are reversed.

The rider spends much time in position right or left with the need to combat the horse's natural crookedness; also because of the frequency of turns, the action of the horse at the canter, and as a preparation for many movements.

8a. Turn on the forehand.   *8b. Leg yield.*   *8c. Shoulder-in.*

LATERAL WORK

Lateral work refers to any form of movement wherein at least one of the horse's hind feet follow in a different track from that of the fore-feet; the horse moving sideways as well as forwards.

The turn on the forehand (page 88). The horse's hind quarters rotate around the forehand, either away from the direction of the bend or, alternatively, in the direction of the bend (Fig. 8a). This exercise is used to teach the rider the use of different leg and rein aids and teaches the horse to move away from the leg.

The rider:

□ Corrects his position.

□ Maintains the walk or halts momentarily.

□ Indicates the direction by asking for a slight bend to the inside.

□ Applies vibrant pressures with his inside leg on the girth. Brings the outside leg slightly further behind the girth, where it can be applied to control the movement if the horse starts to move around too fast.

□ Uses the outside rein to restrain the forward movement and to prevent the horse bending too much in the neck.

□ Turns the body slightly in the direction of the bend. On completing the movement the horse is ridden forward by closing the outside leg and allowing with the hands.

AN ALTERNATIVE: The turn on the forehand ridden in the above manner results in the horse moving his hind quarters away from the direction of the bend. The turn on the forehand can also be executed by reversing the aids, when the rider's outside leg becomes the dominant one to cause the horse to

8d. Travers.   *8e. Renvers.*   *8f. Half-pass.*   *8g. Pirouette.*

step forward and in front of the inside hind leg as in travers (see opposite); the horse then moves the hind quarters in the direction of the bend.

Leg yielding (page 97). In the leg yield the horse is straight, except for a slight bend at the poll, allowing the rider to see the eyebrow and nostril on the inside. This bend is in the opposite direction to that in which he is moving. The inside legs pass and cross the outside legs.

This is the most basic of the lateral movements and can be carried out in walk and working trot. Hence, many riders and/or horses start lateral work with this exercise.

The rider:

□ Corrects his position.

□ Applies the inside leg by the girth. This is the dominant leg, causing the horse not only to step forward but also to bring his inside hind leg further under his body and slightly in front of the other hind leg.

□ Keeps his outside leg just behind the girth and applies when necessary to keep the horse straight and/or to maintain the forward movement.

□ Asks with the inside rein for a slight bend at the poll so that the rider can see the eye and arch of the nostril.

□ Uses the outside rein to regulate the bend to help balance the horse and prevent the shoulder from falling out.

The shoulder-in (page 98). In shoulder-in the horse moves sideways on three or four tracks. He is bent away from the direction in which he is travelling, round the rider's inside leg (Fig. 8c).

The rider:

□ Checks his position.

□ Improves the impulsion and balance with a half-halt.

□ Indicates the bend with the outside rein.

□ Increases the pressure of the inside leg just behind the girth.

□ Contains this extra impulsion by closing the fingers on the opposite (outside) rein, so preventing the horse from stepping straight forward.

□ Rests his outside leg a little further behind the girth than his inside leg to support the bend and stop the hind quarters swinging out, just as on a circle.

□ Turns his body slightly to the inside.

□ Transfers slightly more weight to the inside.

□ Keeps upright and in balance with the horse.

When the shoulder-in is correctly ridden, it should be possible to abandon the inside rein for a few steps without the horse losing his balance, impulsion, or rhythm.

If and when the rider's outside hand allows the horse to move straight forward again, he should do so immediately and return to a circle. However, in a dressage test the horse must be brought back straight on the track.

Travers (quarters-in), and renvers (quarters-out) (page 99). In travers and renvers the horse is bent round the rider's inside leg; the horse looks and moves forward and sideways in the direction in which he is bent. There is little difference between the two: in travers the horse's forehand remains on the track or centre line; in renvers the hind legs remain on the track while the forehand is brought to the inside.

The aids for travers and renvers are identical apart from the original positioning of the horse.

The rider:

□ Checks his position.

□ Improves the balance and impulsion with a half-halt.

□ Asks for a bend with the inside rein and leg.

□ Applies his outside leg behind the girth to move the hind quarters over.

□ Controls the impulsion and the amount of bend with the outside rein.

The half-pass (page 99). This is a variation of travers which is executed on the diagonal. The horse is slightly bent around the inside leg of the rider, and should be aligned as nearly as possible parallel to the long side of the school, but with the forehand slightly in advance of the hind quarters. The horse looks in the direction in which he is going, thus moving both forwards and sideways at the same time. (Fig. 8f.)

The aids are similar to those for travers and renvers.

The rider:

□ Checks his position.

□ Improves the horse's balance and impulsion with a half-halt.

□ Puts the horse into position right, taking the forehand fractionally off the track.

□ Looks and turns his body towards the point to which the movement is being made.

□ Puts more weight into the inside stirrup.

□ Keeps the forward movement and bend with the inside leg.

□ Maintains the bend with the inside rein.

□ Applies the outside leg behind the girth to encourage both the horse's outside legs to step forward and across the front of the two inside legs with rhythmical variations of pressure.

□ Uses the outside rein to control the amount of forward movement and to prevent too much bend.

As the movement progresses, the outside leg aids are gradually increased so that the horse is finally straight (i.e. parallel) to the track or wall before being ridden forward on one track, or before changing to a half-pass on the other rein. The half-pass can be ridden at all three gaits.

The pirouette (pages 100 and 106). This is a circle or half circle performed on two tracks with a radius equal to the length of the horse. The forehand moves around the haunches. The forefeet and the outside hind foot move around the inside hind foot, which acts as the pivot, returning to the same spot or just in front of it each time it is lifted. (Fig. 8g.)

The rider:

☐ Collects the horse by a series of half-halts.

☐ Uses similar aids to those for half-pass, except the length of the stride is adjusted to reduce forward movement and produce a half-pass on the smallest circle.

Pirouettes and half-pirouettes may be ridden at the walk and later at the canter, but can only be achieved at the trot in piaffe.

WORK AT THE CANTER

Counter-canter or contra-lead (page 95). The rider asks the horse to lead with the outside instead of the inside foreleg so that, for example, when circling to the left the horse canters with the right lead.

The rider:

☐ Uses the same aids as for the canter, maintaining the position towards the leading leg so that he will, for example, maintain position left when in counter-canter around a right turn. At first it may be necessary to hold this position more strongly, with the legs definitely applied and the weight positively to the inside, which is on the side of the leading leg.

Change of leg (pages 95-96). To change the leading leg in the canter, the horse can do so through walk and/or trot, or makes a flying change. In a simple change he carries out a transition to the walk and restarts into the canter with the other leg leading. A flying change is completed during the period of suspension in the canter when both fore and hind legs should change together.

Simple change from left canter to right canter (page 95)

The rider:

☐ Checks his position.

☐ Gives the aids to walk.

☐ After the walk has been established, changes his aids from position left to position right and gives the aid to canter right.

TIMING: In the case of a simple change through another gait this is not difficult, but to perform a flying change this must take place during the moment of suspension which follows the use of the horse's leading foreleg. Only then are all four feet off the ground and only then can the horse answer the aids and change the leading hind leg and hence the sequence.

Flying change from left to right (page 96)

The rider:

☐ Checks his position.

44

□ Makes a half-halt to improve the impulsion and balance.
□ Just before the leading leg comes to the ground he changes his aids from position left to position right without collapsing his hips.
□ Makes sure he allows the horse's back muscles to swing.

It is important that the horse is kept straight and that the rider brings the new inside leg forward and the new outside leg back at the same moment.

ADVANCED MOVEMENTS

Piaffe (page 107). This is a highly cadenced, collected, elevated trot on the spot.
The rider:
□ Corrects his position.
□ Uses both legs by the girth, either together or alternatively, to ride forward into a restraining but allowing light rein contact. The object is to ask the horse to bring both hind legs a little further under his body and so to lower his hind quarters and round his back.
□ Sits lightly to allow the horse to round and move 'through' his back, but in an erect position, with the seat bones forward to encourage forward impulsion.
□ As the horse comes into piaffe, indicates the rhythm by increasing and decreasing the pressure of his legs without removing them from the horse's sides. Once the horse has understood, the rider must be careful to take up the rhythm offered by the horse.

A well-trained horse in correct equilibrium will only require a light but consistent contact with the rein to hold it in piaffe, and should always be ready to move straight forward into passage or another gait.
    At an intermediate standard, the horse should be allowed to gain ground, but advanced horses should stay on one spot for 10 to 12 steps.

The passage (page 110). This is a very collected, elevated and cadenced trot. Each diagonal pair of feet is raised higher and with a longer period of suspension than for any other trot.
The rider:
□ Holds both legs firmly against the horse's sides and applies them in the rhythm required. This should encourage the horse to move forward in a slow, supple and highly cadenced trot.
□ Uses the reins to help control the pace and, to a slight degree, the balance.
□ Sits deeply, but softly, in the saddle, in rhythm with the horse's pace so that both rebound together.

PRACTICAL USE OF THE AIDS

The aids and movements can be used in every form of riding. The horse will often be required to carry out some of the schooling movements, not merely as an exercise, or part of a dressage test, but for strictly practical reasons. Thus, when hacking, besides the obvious necessity of the aids for changing direction or altering pace, the turn on the forehand, the pirouette and the rein-back may be used when opening and closing gates, and a rider can help to prevent the horse from shying by using the shoulder-in.

PART 2

Training the Horse

5 The Gaits

INTRODUCTION

To train a horse correctly it is vital to maintain and improve the purity of the gaits rather than to create or fail to correct the numerous defects which develop in the horse's movements. Therefore, the trainer must understand the way the horse should move at the walk, trot, and canter, and for each of these gaits the sequence of the leg movements is different as is the rhythm of the hoof beats.

THE WALK

Rhythm. Four hoof beats should be heard at equal intervals. The horse moves one leg after another so that the four hoof beats can be heard with the same period between each. Two or three feet are always on the ground at the same time, the horse stepping from one foot to another with no moment of suspension.

Sequence in which the legs leave the ground (Fig. 9).
Left hind leg: left foreleg; right hind leg; right foreleg.

The aims
□ Rhythm of hoof beats is regular with the four beats distinctly marked. Any losses of regular four-time hoof beats are incorrect. This includes a

9. The sequence of the footfalls at the walk.

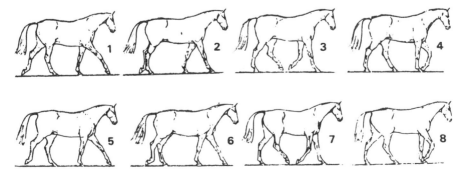

two-time walk (known as a pace or amble).
□ The strides are even and not hurried.
□ The strides are free, purposeful and unconstrained.
□ The head nods in the walk. The rider should not restrict this movement.
□ The legs are lifted, not dragged along the ground.

N.B. Faults in the walk are easily developed, as there is little impulsion to help the rider maintain the rhythm of the pace. It is, therefore, not advisable to walk 'on the bit' during the early stages of training.

THE TROT

Rhythm. Two hoof beats should be heard, with the legs moving in alternate diagonal pairs, but separated by a moment of suspension. This moment of suspension is difficult for the rider to sit to, and the problem can be avoided by rising out of the saddle as one of the diagonal pairs leaves the ground and returning to the saddle as this same pair comes back to the ground (rising trot).

Sequence in which legs leave the ground (Fig. 10)
1. Right foreleg and left hind leg.
2. Left foreleg and right hind leg before the right foreleg and left hind leg touch the ground.

10. The sequence of the footfalls at the trot.

The aims
□ The rhythm of the hoof beats are regular (two-time).
□ The strides are even in length and not hurried.
□ The strides are light and elastic.
□ The hind quarters are engaged.
□ The joints flex and the limbs are not dragged.
□ The hind feet do not hit the forefeet (forgeing).
□ The head remains steady.
The hind legs are as active as the forelegs. The forelegs should not show more extravagant movement than the hind legs; they should not flick and therefore always touch the ground towards which they are pointing so that there is no jerking of the limbs (Fig. 11).

11. Exaggerated action of forelegs in the trot without the corresponding activity of the hind legs.

CANTER

Rhythm. Three hoof beats should be heard and, as with the trot, there is a moment of suspension when all four feet are off the ground.

Sequence in which legs leave the ground (Fig. 12)
When the right foreleg leads:
1. Left hind leg
2. Right hind and left foreleg together
3. Right foreleg followed by a moment of suspension.
When the left foreleg leads:
1. Right hind leg
2. Left hind leg and right foreleg together
3. Left foreleg followed by a moment of suspension.
When the canter is disunited (a fault) the forehand is on one lead and the hind quarters on the other.

The aims
☐ Rhythm of hoof beats is regular (three-time). Four hoof beats should not be heard, but they often are when a horse is slowed down without sufficient impulsion.

12. The sequence of the footfalls at the canter.

☐ Strides are even and not hurried.
☐ Steps are light and cadenced.
☐ Hind quarters are engaged with active hocks.
☐ Balance is maintained.
☐ Horse is straight, with his shoulders directly in front and not to one side of his hind quarters.
☐ The canter is true (not disunited).
☐ Head moves in co-ordination with the horizontal action of the body. The horizontal movement occurs because when only the leading foreleg is on the ground the hind quarters must rise and the head tip towards the ground (see Fig. 12), whereas at the end of the moment of suspension the hind quarters drop and the head rises. The result is a bounding action by the horse in the canter.

GALLOP

Rhythm. This is the horse's fastest and most extended gait: the diagonal sequence of the canter is broken. It thus becomes a pace in which four hoof beats should be heard, followed by a moment of suspension.

Sequence in which legs leave the ground
When the left foreleg leads:
1. Right hind leg
2. Left hind leg
3. Right foreleg
4. Left foreleg followed by a moment of suspension.

The aims
☐ Rhythm of hoof beats is regular (four-time).
☐ Strides are even and not hurried.
☐ Balance is maintained although the centre of gravity is more forward.
☐ Horse is straight with his shoulders directly in front and not to one side of his hind quarters.

VARIATIONS WITHIN A GAIT

A horse can be asked to extend and/or collect (that is, change the length of his strides and outline) at each gait. The extent of the variations within a gait depends upon the stage of the horse's training, and on his own natural ability.

In the initial training, the horse has not the impulsion or suppleness to collect or extend truly: therefore at the trot and canter the working gaits only should be asked for, and in the walk just the medium and free walk. As the training proceeds progressively, more collection can be demanded and at the same time extension, to achieve first of all the medium trot and canter and eventually, the extended walk, trot and canter.

Aims within these variations
□ The collection should result in shorter strides not slow ones, and for the extension longer strides not quick ones. When trying to extend the strides hurrying is one of the commonest faults and leads to stiffening which can spoil the paces. It is nearly always caused by the rider asking the horse to extend before he has enough impulsion to be able to do so.
□ The strides should be even: i.e., when the required length of stride has been achieved each stride should be maintained at this length, so that every stride is *even*.
□ The rhythm of the hoof beats of a particular pace should remain true (the walk four-time, the trot two-time and the canter three-time): i.e. the pace should be *regular*.
□ In all variations within a pace the horse should retain his willingness to go freely forward.

WORKING GAITS (Fig. 13)

These are the gaits which lie between the collected and medium. They are used particularly for horses not yet trained and ready for collected paces. Working walk is not recognised, but the working trot and canter are the gaits from which respectively other trots and canters are developed.

13a. The working trot.   *13b. The working canter.*

Aims at all working gaits
□ To maintain the balance.
□ To keep the horse 'on the bit'.
□ For the hocks to be active, but this does not mean collection, only the production of impulsion from active hind quarters.
□ To produce strides which are free and elastic.

53

14a. The medium walk.   *14b. The medium trot.*

14c. The medium canter.

MEDIUM GAITS (Fig. 14)

These are gaits of moderate extension between working and extended.

Aims at all medium paces
☐ Longer strides than for working, but rounder and shorter than for extended.
☐ Unconstrained strides.
☐ To produce lively impulsion from the hind quarters.
☐ To keep the horse 'on the bit' (*see* pages 81-83) with the head and neck slightly lower than in the working and collected paces. To extend the head more in front of the vertical than in the collected and working gaits.

PARTICULAR FEATURES: At the medium walk the hind feet should touch the ground in front of the footprints of the forefeet (overtracking). This is the walk at which the rider first works the young horse.

EXTENDED GAITS (Fig. 15)

In these the horse lengthens his strides to his utmost.

Aims at all extended paces
☐ The strides to be as long as possible.

15a. The extended walk.   *15b. The extended trot.*

15c. The extended canter.

☐ To produce lively impulsion from the hind quarters.

☐ The horse to remain calm, and light in the forehand.

☐ To keep the horse 'on the bit' with the head and neck lowered and lengthened so that the strides become longer, rather than higher.

☐ Not to make hurried strides.

☐ The rhythm to remain the same.

PARTICULAR FEATURES: At the extended walk, overtracking should be more pronounced than in the medium and the rider should allow the horse to stretch out his head and neck but without losing contact with the mouth. At the extended trot there should be no flicking of the forelegs (Fig. 11).

COLLECTED GAITS (Fig. 16, overleaf)

In these the strides become shorter and higher and the horse is at his most manoeuvrable.

Aims at all collected paces

☐ To produce lively impulsion from the hind quarters, which are strongly engaged with the joints well bent. This should result in a lightening of the forehand and the shoulders becoming more free and mobile.

☐ To keep the horse 'on the bit' with his neck raised and arched so that there is an harmonious curve from the withers to the highest point – the

16a. The collected walk.   *16b. The collected trot.*

16c. The collected canter.

poll. The head should be slightly in front of the vertical but may become more or less perpendicular when the rider uses his aids.
□ The hind legs to be engaged.
□ The quarters should be lowered.

PARTICULAR FEATURES: At the collected walk and trot the hind feet should touch the ground behind or in the footprints of the forefeet.

FREE GAITS

At these the horse is allowed complete freedom to lower and stretch his head and neck. He relaxes, but should remain active. The free walk is the most commonly used, especially for young horses, and as a reward for good work.

6 Lungeing

INTRODUCTION

Lungeing can be used throughout the training of the horse. As long as it is done well it improves the horse's physical co-ordination – developing his rhythm, balance, suppleness, willingness to go forward, and fitness; but probably even more important than this, it trains the horse's mind and can be a major influence on his mental outlook. Through lungeing the horse can be taught to respect, trust and obey his trainer.

Major uses of lungeing are:
☐ The initial training of the young horse.
☐ Retraining spoilt horses.
☐ Exercising horses which are not being ridden.
☐ Settling and relaxing fresh or spirited horses before they are ridden.
☐ Advanced dressage work.
☐ To train the rider. (See Chapter 2.)

Lungeing is therefore a vital aspect of work with horses, but if the horse is to derive full benefit, it demands a trainer with considerable experience, skill and ability to anticipate the horse's movements.

EQUIPMENT

The lungeing area (page 21). An area of flat ground large enough for a circle of at least 20 metres (22 yds). It is an advantage if it is enclosed (sheep hurdles, poles, etc., can be used if an arena is not available), and if it is reasonably quiet so that the horse's attention can be maintained.

Tack
• *A snaffle bridle*, preferably with a simple snaffle bit which has quite a thick single-jointed smooth mouth piece. Either a drop or cavesson noseband is worn. If the reins are not removed they should never be attached to the stirrups or saddle; instead they can be twisted around under the neck and the throat strap put through one of the loops (Fig. 17).
• *A cavesson*. This has a padded noseband with three metal rings attached at the front, and a cheek strap. The cavesson is fitted over the bridle and

17. *The horse tacked up for lungeing. The illustration shows how the reins can be twisted and held by the throat lash.*

can be buckled either under the chin like a drop noseband, or above the bit like a cavesson noseband. The lunge rein is fastened to the central swivel-ring on the noseband. The noseband and cheek strap should be tightened sufficiently to avoid the cheek strap being pulled round to rub the horse's outside eye.

● *A lunge rein* of about 10 metres (33 ft) long, made of linen or nylon webbing with a large loop at one end and a swivel joint attached to a buckle or spring clip at the other.

● *Side-reins*, which should be about 2 metres (6 ft) long, with a clip at one end and a buckle at the other. There should be a large number of holes at the buckle end so that there is scope for varying the length.

● *A roller* with rings on either side to which the side-reins can be attached.

● *A breast plate* to stop the roller or saddle slipping back.

● *A saddle*, possibly with numnah.

● *Boots* that are worn on all four legs to prevent damage to them from knocks.

● *A lungeing whip* with a thong which is long enough to reach the horse.

LUNGEING TECHNIQUE

The trainer. The trainer should wear gloves when lungeing so that if the rein is pulled quickly through his hands it will not burn. He should never wear spurs as these can trip him over.

The trainer who stands correctly will be more efficient and able to react quickly to control the horse who suddenly pulls or turns. In the correct stance:

□ The upper body is erect.

□ The upper arms hang down with the forearms roughly at right angles to the body.

□ The legs are slightly apart.

The lunge rein. This should be held in the hand to which the horse is moving and the whip in the other. The end of the rein is looped (see Fig.

18) so that it can be paid out without tangling, and the loops are held in whichever hand the trainer finds it easier to handle the rein efficiently and without getting it tangled.

18. The first lesson in lungeing, when an assistant can be used.

The position. The trainer stands at an angle of about 35° to 40° to the horse's forehand, with the horse's head just in front of his leading shoulder and himself in line with the horse's hips. He should concentrate on the movement in the horse's hind quarters rather than the forehand, aiming to drive the horse in a circle around him. Control over the hind quarters is vital if the trainer is to prevent the horse stopping or turning. The aim should be for the horse, the whip and the rein to form a triangle. (Fig. 19.)

The horse should describe a true circle, so the trainer aims to stand on one spot, pivoting around one heel. With the young horse, however, in order to remain in control it might be necessary for the trainer to shorten the rein, move closer to the horse and walk in a small circle.

Small circles are a strain for the horse: therefore a young horse should never be asked to describe a circle of less than 20 metres (22 yds) diameter. Only fit, trained horses can be asked to lunge in a smaller circle.

19. Route of horse and trainer, when horse lengthens his stride or jumps on lunge.

THE AIDS

The aim is for these to simulate the aids used when riding. The lunge rein is equivalent to the reins; the whip to the legs, and the voice is used in conjunction with both these aids.

The rein should be used by the trainer to maintain a light, consistent contact with the horse, and the aids should be applied with quick movements of the fingers or, if the horse starts to lean on the rein, by giving and restraining, but not by pulling against him.

The whip is used as an aid, and only in exceptional circumstances as a punishment. The horse should therefore be familiarised with it before lungeing and should learn to accept its being rubbed along his side and hind quarters.

During lungeing the whip can be applied if needed to make the horse move forward or to increase the activity of the hind quarters. It should be flicked just above the hind fetlocks – but quietly; the trainer should not lurch forward and loosen the rein. Normally the threat of the whip with a swing or a crack is sufficient.

The whip is also used to keep the horse out on the circle. If he starts to cut corners or to fall in, it can be pointed and, if necessary, flicked in the direction of his shoulder.

The voice is the aid used most frequently, minimising the use of the whip to make the horse go forward and use of the rein to make him slow down. It is also used to soothe and calm the horse and to help him establish a rhythm to his gaits. The effectiveness of the voice is achieved at first in conjunction with the rein and whip aids so that the horse learns that a sharp quick command 'walk on', 'trot', 'canter', means to move forward, and if low and drawn-out 'whoaa', 'wa-alk', 'ter-rot', to reduce the pace. The tone of the voice is more important than the actual words used.

THE WORK

It is advisable to start on the rein which the horse finds the easier (usually the left) although he should be worked equally on both reins.

The time spent on the lunge will depend largely on his stage of training, his fitness, and the type of work on the lunge – he could walk for a long time but canter for considerably less. As a general rule, five to ten minutes on each rein is sufficient for a green or unfit horse, and as he gets stronger and more balanced this can be gradually increased to a lesson of about ten to fifteen minutes on each rein. The horse must never be overworked: otherwise he will lose his enthusiasm and/or might be physically strained.

THE NOVICE HORSE

As soon as a horse is accustomed to wearing a bridle and cavesson, being led from both sides, and has learned to obey the voice aids to walk on and stand still, then he can be lunged.

For the first lesson he should wear the same tack in which he was led – just a snaffle bridle, cavesson and boots. The lunge rein is attached to the central ring on the cavesson.

Assistance. It is advisable for all but the most experienced trainers to use an assistant during these first lessons. The assistant can then lead the horse from the inside of the circle with the lunge rein running through his hands to the trainer in the centre (Fig. 18). Once the horse has understood that he is supposed to move around in a circle, the assistant can move closer and closer to the trainer, and if the horse stays out, quietly walk out of the way. The same process should be repeated on the other rein.

It can be dangerous for the assistant to lead the horse from the outside.

The halt. When the horse describes a true circle, he must be taught to halt and walk on when commanded. When being led the horse should have learned that 'whoa' and vibrations on the rein mean 'stop'. These same aids should be applied on the lunge, taking care to control the hind quarters with the whip to prevent the horse from turning in towards the trainer. At first this may require the aid of the assistant.

The horse should halt on the track of the circle (although some trainers do ask him to walk in towards them). He should not be asked to remain immobile for more than a few seconds. The trainer should then either ask him to walk on again or go out to him (keeping his whip behind him) to reward with pats, talking and occasional tit-bits.

If the horse does not halt, remember that it may not be through disobedience, but misunderstanding, so be patient. If he persists, work him close to a high ledge or wall (that is unjumpable). If he does not listen to the command to halt/whoa, keep him between the whip and rein to stop him turning in or running down the wall, and direct him towards the wall/high hedge, repeating the command. He will be forced to stop. When he does, make much of him.

The schedule. There can be no time schedule for the lessons below. The horse should master each one in turn, and should be able to remain calm, relaxed and obedient, before progressing to the next. The early lessons should be performed without side reins at a free walk and at a working trot. It is best not to canter until the horse is stronger, but if fresh he can be allowed to canter until he settles sufficiently to pay attention.

The stages
- *Lungeing with a roller.* The roller is fitted as on page 68, and the horse

61

is lunged with it in place. The horse has to learn to relax and move freely with this restriction around his back and belly.

● *Lungeing with a saddle.* When the horse is relaxed with a roller it can be replaced by a saddle. At first the stirrups should be removed. In a later lesson they can be run up, and finally before he is backed can be allowed to hang free for a short time so that the horse gets used to being touched where the rider's legs will be.

● *Lungeing with side-reins.* These are attached to either the roller or the saddle a little above half way up the horse's side (Fig. 20). To prevent them slipping down, the rings on the roller are preferable attachments. Before attaching them to the bit, the side-reins are made as long as possible and of equal length, then crossed over at the withers and attached to the Ds on the saddle or roller. The horse is then lunged for a few minutes on both reins to supple up and relax.

The side-reins are then unclipped, and most trainers then attach them directly on to the bit, but some recommend attaching them to the side rings on the cavesson for the first lessons. The horse is then lunged with the side-reins so loose that he cannot feel their effect.

When he works calmly and rhythmically (it might be during that lesson or two or three later), the side-reins can be shortened, but making sure that they both remain of an equal length.

The side-reins should be adjusted to such a length that the horse makes contact with them when he engages his hind quarters, rounds his back and lowers his head. The aim is that as the horse has made the contact himself he will not fear it but will soon start to seek it and to chew gently at the bit.

20. Side reins (left) correctly fitted ; (right) too short.

The side-reins should not be used to pull the horse's head into a particular position, nor should they be so tight that his head comes behind the vertical (Fig. 20, right). The horse's state of balance and way of going must always dictate their length. It is also dangerous for the horse to walk much with the side-reins attached, as they restrict the natural movement of his head and make it more difficult to maintain the correct rhythm of the pace.

As the horse's balance improves he can bring his hind legs further underneath him, his outline becomes shorter and rounder, and the side-reins slacken. This is the time to shorten the side-reins, but never so much that the horse stiffens and resists against them.

Some trainers only use the side-reins for a brief period when familiarising the horse with the contact of the bit, before backing. They prefer to give the horse the freedom both to find his own balance and to stretch forward and down. This also avoids the danger of the horse resisting the contact by either hollowing his back and raising his head (above the bit) or getting over-bent and falling behind the contact (behind the bit).

Straightness. Young horses are not straight (see page 80) but lunge work with side-reins helps to reduce crookedness. This is not achieved by shortening the inside rein, which only swings the hind quarters to the outside, throwing the weight on to the inside shoulder and tending to make him want to bend to the outside and resist.

If the side-reins are kept at the same length, when the horse places his inside hind leg well under him, which he must do to turn in a circle, his weight will be transferred diagonally towards the outside shoulder. To maintain his balance he will turn his head and neck to the inside. The pressure on the outside rein becomes stronger and the mouth becomes moist on that side, whereas the inside rein becomes looser.

Variations of gait and gaits. The horse can be encouraged to extend the length of his trot stride to do some medium trot, and this is easiest for him if he is driven out of the circle on to a straight line and then returned into a circle in a different place, when he can be brought back again into the working trot. (Fig. 19.)

The canter is introduced when the horse can trot with rhythm, has a willingness to go forward, and moves with a supple swinging back. Its introduction should be a gradual process, the trainer asking at first for just a few strides on both reins. It is usually advisable to remove the side reins for early lessons at the canter.

It is important for the trainer to recognise if faults are occurring at any of the gaits (i.e. four-time canter). He should aim to improve the horse's gaits all the time, and to do this must have a clear picture of what is correct. (See Chapter 5.)

Backing. A horse which is calm when wearing a saddle and accepts the bit happily at the trot can be backed, but the more time spent on the lunge, the easier it will be for the rider to train the horse. It is, however, advisable for the horse to learn to accept the weight of the rider before he gets too fit and strong. Many trainers therefore back him while continuing with training on the lunge: i.e., lunge him for fifteen to twenty-five minutes before he is ridden or alternate days of lungeing with days of riding.

LUNGEING OVER OBSTACLES

Lungeing over poles. This helps to give variety to the work and encourages the young horse to lower his head, round his back and flex his joints.

The side-reins are always removed for this work and for all jumping.

The horse is first led over the pole, and if he remains relaxed is then lunged at the walk and trot on a circle which is just short of the pole. When he relaxes he can be driven out of the circle and over the pole.

When lungeing over obstacles the trainer must ensure that:
☐ The horse is presented straight at the pole and does not approach it at an acute angle which would encourage him to run out. This means that the trainer will have to move at right angles to the pole and the horse will no longer describe a circle. (Fig. 19)
☐ The horse is given as much freedom as possible over the pole and is not restricted by the lunge rein from lowering his head.
☐ The horse is driven from behind. The trainer should never get in front of him.
☐ The work is done in equal amounts on both reins.
☐ The trainer allows the horse to take a number of straight strides upon landing and is not pulled straight back into a circle.
When the horse walks and trots in a relaxed manner over this single pole in both directions, the exercise can be extended. Poles over which he can be lunged can be scattered around the school or laid in a series either in a straight line or round in a circle. They should be about 1.2 to 1.3 metres (4-4½ ft) apart. (See page 116.) It is important for them to remain at the correct distance, and if a pole is displaced by the horse the poles should not be attempted again until correctly positioned. Heavy poles help to prevent this occurrence.

Lungeing over raised poles. When the horse trots over the poles in a relaxed manner, maintaining his rhythm and lowering his head, raised poles on blocks can be introduced. The same techniques are used as for poles on the ground (i.e. leading over, using single ones first and progressing to a series).

Lungeing over a jump. Ideally the wing stands of the fence should be low. A pole should be leant against the inside jump stand to prevent the lunge rein being fouled and to act as a wing (Fig. 21). With the poles on the ground the horse is led over the jump.

The horse is then lunged over the jump with the poles on the ground. When he does this calmly and without rushing, the end of the pole nearest to the trainer can be raised. When the horse is happy trotting over this, another pole can be added to make a cross bar, and after this a third bar laid along the top, and later a fourth bar to make a parallel.

It is important to make the jumping fun for the horse so that the progress

21. A well-prepared obstacle for lungeing.

should be gradual. He should not be asked too much nor should the lessons be too long.

MORE ADVANCED WORK ON THE LUNGE

The main purposes of lungeing more advanced horses are:

□ As a means of loosening up horses which, in their preliminary work, stiffen against the weight of the rider.

□ As a visual aid to the trainer, who can study from the ground whether his horse is going straight, has sufficient impulsion and suppleness, and that the gaits are true.

□ As an aid to collection at the trot and canter. The horse can be gradually brought on to smaller and smaller circles (but never so small that he loses his rhythm or his back stops swinging), while the trainer asks for as much impulsion as possible. Then while maintaining this collection the horse is allowed to go back on to a larger circle.

□ As an aid to extension at the trot. The horse can be brought into a collected trot, then driven out of the circle on to a straight line, in the same manner as medium trot was asked for in *Variations of gait* on page 63.

□ Teaching piaffe (and very occasionally passage) in hand. This work is carried out on straight lines and is described on pages 107-109.

7 The Initial Training of the Horse

INTRODUCTION

In the horse's natural state his instinctive defence is flight, and he only fights if provoked. The aim of early training is to overcome his fear, to earn his trust and obedience, and to turn the instinct of flight into a willingness to go forward at all times.

Efforts to do this should start from the time a foal is born, and if they are successful in the early stages they will greatly simplify the horse's subsequent training.

EARLY HANDLING

A foal should be handled from birth so that he learns to trust and respect humans and not to fear them. In the years before he is ridden he should be trained progressively to:
□ Lead quietly.
□ Be halter broken and tied up.
□ Be groomed and have his feet picked out and trimmed.
□ Accept the various items of tack used for breaking and riding.
□ Become familiar with and learn not to fear a variety of strange sights and sounds.
□ Obey the basic commands: i.e., 'walk on', 'whoa'.

INITIAL TRAINING

When the horse is three or four years old he should have developed sufficiently – physically and mentally – to undergo the concentrated and progressive training of being backed, ridden and learning the aids.

THE STAGES OF TRAINING:
1. Leading in hand.
2. Lungeing.
3. Backing: i.e., teaching the horse to accept a rider on his back.
4. Being ridden on the lead and lunge.
5. Control by the rider.

Feeding during these stages must be carefully monitored. A young horse full of oats tends to be too spirited to understand and obey. It is vital to keep him sensible, which usually means limiting his feed (unless he is lazy and/or weak), and turning him out to grass whenever possible.

The length of training varies from horse to horse, depending largely on the horse's temperament, the extent and success of his initial handling, and the ability of the trainer.

As a rough guide, and assuming that the early handling of the foal has been satisfactory, a professional trainer usually takes four to six weeks to lead, lunge, back and quietly ride a young horse. This applies to training at a school where cost, and therefore time, is usually an important factor.

It is essential for training not to be hurried. The horse should never be asked to carry out more than his condition or temperament warrant. Anyone wishing to train their own horse would be well advised to spend much longer on this early work. Extensive work on the lunge pays dividends later on, and up to twelve weeks can be spent on this stage.

TACK (see also pages 57-58)

The following tack is needed:
□ A lungeing cavesson.
□ A snaffle bridle.
□ A linen or nylon webbing lunge rein.
□ A roller and breast plate.
□ A saddle, preferably with numnah and breast plate.
□ Side-reins.
□ Boots which should be worn on all four legs in all work.
□ A neck strap, if a breast plate is not fitted.
The trainer needs a long lunge whip and should always wear gloves.

Fitting the tack. The items should be introduced one at a time, the horse being allowed to accept each new item quietly and calmly before another is tried.

To fit a lunge cavesson. This should be buckled tightly enough to avoid it being pulled around. The lead/lunge rein is normally fitted to the central ring of the cavesson.

To fit a bridle. The snaffle bit must fit the horse's mouth so that it is neither so narrow that it pinches, nor so wide that the joint falls far down in the horse's mouth. The mouth piece should be quite thick and single-jointed. Some horses object to having a bridle fitted, however carefully this is done, and in such cases the bridle may be put on like a head collar with the bit fastened to the off-side cheek piece only and allowed to hang down. The bit can then be put in the horse's mouth very gently before securing the near-side cheek piece tightly enough so that corners of the horse's mouth just wrinkle.

If the bit is too low the horse can easily get his tongue over it, if too high it will be uncomfortable.

To fit a cavesson over the bridle. See pages 57-58.

To fit a roller. Great care is necessary when first fitting a roller and later the saddle, as many horses are very disturbed by the restrictive feeling of the girth. One person is needed to hold the horse's head, also to help with adjustments on the horse's off-side if a third person is not available. The trainer stands on the near-side and places the roller, with the buckle end bent back over itself, very gently on the horse's back. The breast plate is attached to prevent the roller from slipping back, before the buckle end of the girth is gently slid down the horse's off-side, quietly brought under the horse, and drawn up to the retaining straps on the roller. It is attached very loosely at first, but if the horse is not upset it is gradually tightened by one or two holes at a time. It is advisable to move the horse forward a few steps between each tightening operation.

To fit a saddle. The same procedure is followed as for fitting the roller, including the attachment of the breast plate. Initially it is important for the girth to be only just tight enough to prevent the saddle from slipping; if too tight the horse will often buck against the pressure.

LEADING IN HAND

The foal. In most cases a horse is taught to lead in and out of his field or stable alongside his dam. To start with, the foal should be walked around his stable with a stable rubber around his neck, and a hand around his hind quarters. It is important to push rather than pull, helping to instil the willingness to go forward at an early age. Once he understands this, he may be led from a foal slip, but one hand should remain on or around the hind quarters, and it is this hand which deals with any arguments. The foal will soon learn that it is useless to resist and may then be led outside his stable, following his mother.

The young horse. If a young horse has missed this early training he can be taught to lead in a stable, preferably a large one, and it is best not to lead him outside until he is quiet and obedient on both reins.

A young horse should be led by a rein of about 3 metres (10 ft) fastened to the central ring of a lunge cavesson. When the horse is used to a bridle, one may be fitted under the cavesson, but the lead rein should never be

22a. Use of the whip when horse is reluctant to be led forward.

attached to the snaffle bit as this may spoil his mouth.

Assistance. In the early stages, unless the horse has been taught to move freely forward as a foal, it is advantageous for the trainer to have an assistant walking behind the horse. He can then send the horse forward if he tries to stop or run back.

Technique. The trainer should walk alongside, but not in front, of the horse's shoulder on the near-side, holding a whip in his left hand, which should be long enough to reach the hind quarters. If the horse draws back, or tries to stop, he can use his voice and the whip behind his back (Fig. 22a). Often the threat of the whip is sufficient to make the horse obey, but if necessary it can be applied gently and, if not effective, more strongly.

Forward movement is of prime importance in the early and indeed all stages of training. If, however, the young horse tries to hurry or run on too much, repeated, rapid jerks on the front of the cavesson, together with the voice, can be used to slow him down or stop.

When the horse accepts being led on the near-side he should be taught to go equally well from the off-side.

Before starting to lunge, the horse should obey the commands to 'walk on' and 'whoa'.

LUNGEING

Lungeing has a vital part to play in the training of the young horse, as long as it is carried out correctly. The previous chapter described in detail the technique of lungeing.

LONG REINING

In the past, long reining was widely practised as an alternative or supplement to lungeing, before backing was carried out. Although it enables a higher standard of training to be achieved, it requires special skills, and needs an experienced trainer if the young horse is not to be spoilt. The novice trainer should not experiment with long reining on a young horse, but should first learn the technique under the guidance of an expert, using an older horse as a guinea pig.

The stages

1. The horse is tacked up as for lungeing, with bridle, roller, cavesson, to which the lunge rein is attached on the central ring, and boots. The trainer carries a lunge whip and first settles the horse, lungeing him in the normal manner.
2. With the trainer holding the lunge rein and standing by the horse's inside shoulder, an assistant attaches a second lunge rein to the side ring on the outside of the cavesson, runs it back through the D on the roller and around the outside of the horse's hind quarters. This must be carried out with great care so that the horse will not be frightened by the feel of the rein. With a nervous horse, some people begin with the rein coming from the D over the horse's back, and progress from there to round the quarters.
3. The trainer is given the second (outside) rein but does not place any tension on this rein until the horse is calm and relaxed. The horse is asked to go forward in a circle around the trainer as on the lunge, with the inside rein acting as a normal lunge rein.
4. The inside rein is attached to the inside ring of the cavesson and run back through the D on the roller as with the outside rein. In work gradually more pressure is put on the outside rein to develop it as a controlling aid.
5. The horse is asked to change direction, at the walk, the previous outside rein becoming the inside one.
6. The reins are attached to the bit instead of the cavesson.
7. The horse is asked to go forward in straight lines and to turn corners with the trainer behind him.

Whether on a circle or a straight line, the horse can be asked to halt, move off and change his gait.

The time schedule for these stages depends on the temperament of the horse and on how advanced his training is. The vital factor is that the trainer only attempts the next stage if the horse is calm in the easier work. Long reining is usually of greatest value in advanced dressage work, as it is a useful aid to achieving collection and lateral work.

BACKING

Timing. The trainer must decide when a horse is ready to be backed, according to each individual case. It is generally not attempted until the horse is obedient, relaxed and working well on the lunge.

If the preparatory work has been carried out correctly, the horse should accept the rider quietly and with confidence. Conversely, a horse who reacts violently to being backed has almost certainly been inadequately prepared.

Equipment. Backing is best carried out in an enclosed place, such as an indoor riding school or a small paddock. The horse should be fitted with a snaffle bridle under the cavesson, a breast plate, and a saddle, which most trainers prefer without stirrup leathers and irons.

Assistance. If possible, three people should be available: the trainer, who usually holds the horse; an assistant, who helps the rider to mount and dismount and to maintain his position on the saddle; and the rider. With an experienced trainer, however, backing can – and often has to be – achieved by two people. The trainer then both helps the rider to mount and holds the horse.

A useful aid is to place a straw bale by the horse for the rider to use as a mounting block and to help accustom the horse to seeing a human above him.

The stages

1. Before starting, the horse should be lunged to settle him. When he is relaxed and calm, he should be led on the left rein alongside a wall or fence, but about a metre away, and halted. The trainer stands at the horse's head, on the near-side, holding him by the lunge rein which is attached to the cavesson. The rider, also on the near-side, takes hold of the saddle, pats it, moves it gently about on the horse's back, jumps up and down a few times and then repeats this with one hand on the pommel and the other on the cantle. The whole procedure should then be repeated on the off-side.

2. If the horse remains calm, the trainer, or his assistant if he has one, can give the rider a leg up so that he can lean across the saddle (Fig. 22b). This exercise is then repeated on the off-side. If the horse becomes upset, the trainer should comfort him and the rider can slide quietly to the ground. Whenever possible, the rider, whilst lying across the saddle, pats the horse on the opposite side. To reach this stage on the first day of backing is sufficient progress.

3. When the young horse accepts the rider leaning across the saddle from either side, he can be led forward a few steps – but this position is tiring for the rider and cannot be held for long.

4. The rider can then start to move around a little on the saddle, both at the halt and as the horse is led forward. He can also slowly raise his head and shoulders.

5. As the horse becomes confident, the rider can put a leg over the saddle, taking care not to touch the horse's hind quarters, to sit astride. The top

22b. Legging up the rider to lean across the saddle.

part of the rider's body is still kept low, near to the horse's neck. This is done at the halt, and when the horse remains calm he can be walked forward a few paces. The rider can then slowly raise his body so that the horse becomes used to him sitting upright.

At all times the rider and the trainer must be quick to reward the horse when he does well, by patting him on the neck and praising him. Titbits should be avoided except as a reward at the end of the lesson.

RIDING ON THE LEAD AND LUNGE

When first ridden the horse is led forward quietly, with the rider sitting upright but relaxed. Control is in the hands of the person leading, who can pay out the rein and move away until the horse is on the lunge circle.

When the horse walks the circle calmly he can be asked to trot: at first when being led and then on the lunge. The rider starts in sitting trot with very little weight on the seat bones, but uses the rising trot as soon as his coming out of the saddle does not alarm the horse.

Equipment. Stirrups are used at the discretion of the rider; some prefer to use them from the start – but with caution, as they can get in the way and upset the horse by banging on his sides. The neck strap or breast plate is always worn and can be used by the rider to secure his position without interfering with the horse's mouth. The reins should be attached to the bit from the beginning, but only used in dire emergencies. Side-reins should never be fitted.

Introducing the aids. If the horse remains calm when being led around the school or paddock with the rider on his back, the aids can be introduced. The trainer, holding the lunge rein loosely, should encourage the horse to walk and halt, first in obedience to his voice and then to the rider's. The rider can then begin to introduce the rein and leg aids in conjunction with his voice. A schooling whip should be carried by the rider to reinforce when necessary (but with great care) the leg aids.

CONTROL BY THE RIDER

When the horse walks, trots, and halts calmly to the rider's aids, the lunge rein can be removed. To ensure a smooth changeover after detaching the rein, the trainer continues to walk beside the horse, although leaving control to the rider, before moving away gradually.

The rider should concentrate on getting his horse to move forward calmly in answer to his aids, including the voice. When he wishes to make a turn he will have to rely on the use of the reins alone, moving a hand out boldly to the required side, but without any backward tension and still riding the horse forward.

Quiet, clear commands and firm but kind handling should produce results, with the horse obeying the simple aids at walk and trot.

Cantering. There should be no hurry to teach the horse to canter with a rider. If started too early it can excite the young horse and may result in his losing his balance, even to the extent that the sequence of the pace and the length of stride is impaired.

To begin with, cantering should only be asked for on a straight line. On corners the horse should be allowed to fall back into the trot until repetition improves his balance and understanding of what is wanted. The rider merely takes up the correct position and gives encouragement until later when the more serious cantering lessons can start.

It is often easier for a young horse to canter if the rider adopts the basic position for jumping (page 17).

Standing still when mounted. For safety and discipline it is essential for the horse to remain still when mounted, both when the rider is legged up and when he uses the stirrup.

An assistant trainer should hold the horse's head to ensure that he does not move when the rider is legged up and first learns to accept the rider mounting with a foot in the stirrup. These first lessons are best carried out at the end of a riding session so that the horse is relaxed and even a little tired.

73

As soon as the horse is not disturbed by this manner of mounting, the rider can mount using the stirrups at the beginning of a session, at first with an assistant holding the head, but after a few days without him. Then the rider must keep the horse immobile through use of the voice and, if necessary, the reins.

Acceptance of strange objects. An essential part of a young horse's training is to get him to accept strange sights and sounds without fear. Even when he is a foal, coloured poles can be placed on the ground at the entrance to his paddock and he can be encouraged to follow his dam over them. It is beneficial, too, to turn him out in a field from which traffic can be seen and heard.

TRAFFIC. Motor vehicles are a serious hazard today and great care must be taken to train the young horse to accept them calmly. It is important to take every possible precaution to prevent him from being frightened by lorries or cars. When riding outside for the first few times it is advisable to go with one or two trained quiet horses who can set an example and give confidence. At first the trained horse should be kept between the young horse and the traffic, and if he remains calm, the older horse can go in front of him, and eventually behind.

SHYING. If a horse shies at an object, he should not be beaten or forced too close to it, but allowed to pass by at what he considers a safe distance and with his head bent away from it. If each time he passes the object causing concern, the rider can quietly ask him to go a little nearer, the horse should eventually overcome his fear to pass it without shying. In this way any argument can be avoided, and it is more likely that the cure will be permanent.

SUMMARY

When a young horse is able to walk, trot, and canter calmly under the control of his rider, and has had regular ridden exercise for two to three months, he should be sufficiently confident and physically fit to undertake the next stage of training. This is explained in Chapter 8, 'The Basic Training of the Horse'.

8 The Basic Training of the Horse

INTRODUCTION

A horse which has completed the training covered in Chapter 7, 'The Initial Training of the Horse', should be moving freely forward, calmly and on a comparatively long rein in all three gaits. The training in this chapter will help the horse to develop mentally and physically, increasing the scope of his natural ability so that he becomes a more pleasant ride and a better horse for competitions. It is training that can be used to improve the performance of every type of horse.

The basic training of the horse
☐ Stimulates his willingness to go forward.
☐ Develops his natural abilities.
☐ Strengthens his physique.
☐ Makes him more supple and gymnastic.
☐ Increases his stamina.
☐ Gives the rider more control.

GENERAL PRINCIPLES

The following are important:
• *Avoidance of short cuts*. Training requires time, effort and patience. Short cuts, such as the use of gadgets, should be avoided as these develop resistances and create their own problems.
• *Rate of progress*. Training cannot be conducted to a time-scale; it must be dependent on the progress made. The rate of progress will vary according to the ability and temperament of the horse and the rider. Although the trainer plans a programme for progressive training, it must be sufficiently flexible to suit the individual characteristics of the horse being trained.
• *Use of reward and punishment*. The following system of training uses rewards and punishments, but no force, to teach the acceptance of the aids and obedience to the rider. The amount of reward and punishment will vary according to the character of the horse. Hot-blooded, high-spirited horses usually need more rewards than lazy horses, who may benefit from occasional reprimands. The trainer must analyse the character of his horse and apply the appropriate discipline. In all cases persuasion is

recommended as being more effective than coercion. A frightened horse is too tense to learn. The aim must be willing co-operation obtained by rational and tactful methods, but at the same time there must never be any doubt as to who is in command; if authority and respect are lost, training stops.

THE TRAINER/RIDER

Since it is the rider who trains the horse it will be assumed throughout this chapter that the trainer is the rider.

Qualities of a good trainer
□ Ability to make the horse understand. If the horse does not obey, the trainer must consider whether his instructions were understood. Before blaming the horse he should examine his aids and methods.
N.B. If a good basic position has been established by the trainer the aids can be given more clearly.
□ An understanding of the general nature of a horse and an ability to adapt his approach according to the temperament and individual characteristics of the horse he is training.
□ Patience and persistence.
□ Temper must always be controlled.
□ An air of calm authority when with the horse: ensuring that all movements are quiet and deliberate.
□ Tolerance of playful high spirits in in a young horse, but firmness in the face of wilful disobedience.
□ A good sense of rhythm.
□ A sufficient knowledge of horsemastership in order to ensure that his horse is being well cared for and suitably fed.

EQUIPMENT

This should include:
□ A snaffle bridle with a drop, flash or cavesson noseband.
□ A long schooling whip which can be used to reinforce leg aids.
□ Brushing boots to be worn on all four legs.
□ An enclosed area, preferably on good going for flat work.

OBJECTIVES OF TRAINING

The following objectives are the basis of all training. It is difficult to place them in order of priority because they are inter-related, with improvements to one being dependent upon – and having repercussions on – other objectives. Also, as methods of achieving them overlap, several may be worked on simultaneously. As each horse has different strengths and weaknesses the importance of work on a particular objective will vary.

The seven objectives are:

1. Controlled forward impulsion.
2. Rhythm and balance.
3. Suppleness.
4. Straightness.
5. Acceptance of the bit.
6. Submission.
7. Development of the gaits.

CONTROLLED FORWARD IMPULSION

'Impulsion is a tendency to move forward with elasticity, originating from the haunches, flowing into a swinging back and ending in the mouth' (Colonel Handler). It is contained energy created by the activity of the hind quarters and should be instantly ready for the rider to call on. The consequent willingness and ability of the horse to go forward is the foundation of all work. If impulsion is lost it should be recreated before other movements are attempted.

N.B. *Impulsion is not speed.* A horse which has impulsion should be able to establish a slower rhythm to his gaits.

To develop impulsion. The first step is to achieve the basis of impulsion – the willingness to go forward. Until the horse goes forward to the aids it will be difficult to control him (a stationary horse cannot be steered and a lazy/slow one only with difficulty).

The horse must therefore be made responsive to the leg – to be in front of the leg. Leg aids can, if necessary, be supported by the voice and taps with the whip. As the training progresses and the horse gains his rhythm and balance, more forward momentum can be created and the seat aids can be brought into action. This forward momentum, instead of producing more speed, can be partly contained within the horse (impulsion). The driving aids, rather than simply making him go forward can – if the rider's hands restrain but allow – result in the horse's hind quarters becoming more engaged and active. This gives the horse the power to go forward as soon as he is asked.

In creating this forward impulsion it is important for it not to be associated with speed. He should never be asked to go forward so much that he begins to lose balance and goes faster, nor should so much impulsion be created that the rider cannot control it, for then the tendency is to pull the reins backwards, which destroys the impulsion and creates resistance.

RHYTHM AND BALANCE

Rhythm is the regular recurrence of a given time interval between one footfall and the next in any of the paces. Each pace has its own rhythm. The walk is four-time (1-2-3-4), the trot is two-time (1-2, 1-2), and the canter three-time (1-2-3).

N.B. Tempo should be distinguished from rhythm. It is the speed of the rhythm: the time it takes for a sequence of the footfalls to occur. Cadence is when a pace has pronounced rhythm. (See *Improvement of the Gaits*, page 84.)

Importance of rhythm. As in so many other spheres of activity (athletics, ballet, etc.) rhythm is vital to make best use of ability. When a horse has rhythm he will also be balanced and will find it easier to remain calm and relaxed. Many trainers believe that rhythm is the clearest and easiest primary objective. When it is achieved the horse should be balanced, calm and relaxed.

To develop rhythm. The aim is to get a horse to maintain the rhythm of a particular pace on circles, straight lines and through corners. To do this he must be balanced.

When a horse is moving freely in his paddock he has natural balance, but when he starts to be ridden the weight of the rider puts him on his forehand. If he maintains his natural balance this will make it difficult to keep a rhythm. The hind legs will tend to push the weight rather than lift it, which will usually make the gaits flat, heavy and irregular. To be balanced, in a rhythm when carrying a rider, the horse has to engage his hind legs, bringing them further underneath his and the rider's body. To achieve this, the rider applies short but repeated aids with legs, and later with the seat, asking the horse to go forward to a restraining but allowing hand (half-halts). At the same time the rider must think of the rhythm of the gait.

SUPPLENESS

A horse must be supple in order to be a comfortable ride and to make best use of his physique. The aim is a suppleness which allows the relaxed co-ordination of every muscle and joint. Tension is the major restriction on such an aim – for whether it is caused by excitement, apprehension, or resistance, it not only reduces concentration but it also inhibits freedom of movement. To be supple the horse should be calm and relaxed. The most common area of tension is the back – for the horse naturally tends to stiffen and become rigid under the weight of the rider. This makes it difficult for the rider to sit in the saddle, to apply his seat aids and to feel the actions of the horse, and for the aids to come 'through'. (See *Submission*, page 83.)

The horse's back muscles should be supple and should 'swing' so that the muscles behind the saddle move in unison with the horse's legs to provide an elastic connection, and so co-ordinate the hind quarters and the forehand. At the walk, sitting trot and canter, the trainer must be supple enough not to impede the horizontal and vertical movement in the horse's back. (See pages 16-17.)

To develop suppleness. The horse has to be suppled both laterally and longitudinally.

TO SUPPLE HIM LATERALLY he must learn to bend round the rider's inside leg. This is achieved by working through circles, loops and serpentines, and later, in lateral work, particularly shoulder-in. He must not be allowed to increase the weight on the inside rein and must be encouraged to engage the inside hind leg. Care must be taken that the amount of bend asked for is equal on both reins.

TO SUPPLE HIM LONGITUDINALLY means that:

☐ He brings his hind legs more underneath his body.

☐ He learns to lift and swing his back.

☐ He makes his top line rounder by lengthening the muscles along his back and neck.

This is most easily done on large circles. The horse is ridden from the inside leg into the outside rein and encouraged with half-halts to work in a rounder manner. The horse should soon start to lower his head, going forward to the hand, with the rider encouraging greater engagement of the hind quarters. The rider must allow this 'working down' and not restrict the swinging back muscles with his seat or block with his reins. The rhythm and impulsion must be maintained otherwise the horse will go on to his forehand and the whole object of the exercise will be lost.

Other important suppling exercises are: frequent well-executed transitions, encouragement of the willingness to go forward, use of trotting poles and small fences and, later, lateral work.

23. A horse basculing over a parallel fence.

STRAIGHTNESS

The horse is straight when the hind legs follow the tracks of the forelegs, which means when moving on straight lines he will be straight and on curved lines slightly bent from nose to tail along the line of the curve. There should not be any greater bend in the neck than in the rest of the body.

To make the horse straight. The untrained horse is rarely straight and the rider will feel that the horse accepts the rein contact more readily on one side than on the other. The hind leg will bend more on the hollow side and will not truly follow the track of the corresponding foreleg. Therefore, the shorter muscles on the hollow side have to be lengthened gradually, to avoid strain and stress. Forcible bending of the neck produces tension, resistance and tilting of the head. It is important to avoid concentrating entirely on the forehand, as the hind leg which is slightly left behind must be encouraged to come forward and under the body.

It is difficult to make a horse truly straight until he is capable of performing the best of all straightening exercises – the shoulder-in. By this stage, too, the hind quarters will be more engaged and the shoulders easier to control: therefore not too much emphasis should be placed on straightening the young horse. The following is excellent preliminary work.

If the horse is stiff to the right and hollow to the left he will be slightly bent in his whole body around the rider's left leg and may tend to bend his neck too much to that side and will drop the inside rein. With such a horse the trainer begins his schooling sessions riding on the left rein (which is the easier for the horse) and concentrates at first in preventing him from bending his neck too much to the left. Contact with the left rein is maintained while using short, gentle taking-and-giving actions with the right rein to reduce the excess bend in the neck. At the same time the trainer uses his leg (and seat) aids to push the horse forward into the hand to obtain an even and momentarily stronger contact. (A very green horse will rarely take enough contact to do this). It is important – as with all work – for the use of the seat and leg aids and the maintenance of the will to go forward to be kept uppermost in the mind during these straightening exercises. An excess of rein aids leads to resistance and the horse dropping behind the aids.

After several circuits the rider should change the bend and repeat the same lesson on the more difficult rein for the horse. On this rein the rider asks for more bend by riding from the inside leg into a still, outside rein, using taking-and-giving aids with the inside rein. Equal amounts of work should be done on both reins.

N.B. The rider should gradually experience a more even feel on the reins and have less difficulty in correcting the bend in the neck, but it is a slow process, as muscles must develop to enable the horse to get straighter. The aids for correcting a stiffness to the right should be reversed if the horse is stiff to the left.

The problem of one-sided stiffness has to be dealt with throughout the training of most horses. At times the feel on both reins may be the same, even then the following day slight stiffness on one side may be felt.

ACCEPTANCE OF THE BIT

The horse accepts the bit when he maintains a light elastic rein contact with the rider without resistance and with submissiveness throughout his body. When jumping, riding out, or in early stages of training, he may accept the bit without fulfilling the conditions necessary to be 'on the bit'.

A horse is on the bit if:
☐ The hocks are correctly placed.
☐ The neck is more or less raised and arched, according to the stage of training and the extension or collection of the pace.
☐ He accepts the bit without resistance, with a light and soft contact, a relaxed jaw, and submissiveness throughout his body.
☐ The head remains steady and, as a rule, slightly in front of the vertical.
☐ A supple poll is the highest point of the neck.

The rein contact should not be hard and solid, nor should it be so light that it is like holding a thread. A correct contact means a consistent elastic easy tension that comes from a forward tendency originating in the hind quarters and passes 'through' a relaxed and swinging back, the neck and so to the mouth, where it is accepted evenly on both sides. Such a contact is only possible when the horse is in balance, carrying himself and not relying on support from the reins. Balance and contact are therefore complimentary – the better the balance, the better the contact, and vice versa.

To accept the bit, the horse should be:
● *Worked* so that he develops a constant willingness and ability to go forward (impulsion).
● *Trained* so that he is straight and accepts the same contact on either side of his mouth.
● *Encouraged* to 'seek the bit' from quite an early stage of his education.

The trainer should, as soon as possible, take a light but positive and continuous contact with the bit through the reins. By keeping the horse calm and in rhythm, using an 'asking' leg and 'allowing' hand, but without losing contact, the rider should soon induce the horse to move forward on to the bit. The horse can be allowed to carry his head in a natural position as long as the rider follows the mouth to maintain a light contact, with a forward, not pulling, tension through the reins. The rider should, in effect say: 'this is my hand and you must accept it', so the horse finds that the

81

hand is acceptable and there is no point in resisting it.

The horse uses his head and neck to balance himself, so the trainer should never use the reins to place the head in a particular position. A horse will carry his head in accord with his conformation, the stage of training he has reached, the flexibility of all his joints and the activity on his hind quarters.

If the horse pulls on the reins in an effort to go faster, the trainer, with many downward transitions and repeated taking-and-giving actions of the reins, should make him accept a balance and rhythm on a lighter contact.

If the horse is above the bit (Fig. 24) his head is held high, the angle of the head is too far in front of the vertical and his back tends to hollow. Such a horse should be given exercises to develop a stronger and more rounded back. (See *To develop suppleness*, page 79.) He is usually best worked at the rising trot, or in bad cases, at the walk. The rein contact should be particularly sympathetic, the rider trying to feel with his hand, encouraging the horse to bend his poll, relax his lower jaw and stop resisting the contact. The horse should be ridden forward to a rein contact and asked to engage his hind quarters which will encourage him to round his back and lower his head. This is especially effective when working on a circle when the trainer can ride positively to the outside rein asking intermittently with an open inside rein for the bend and allowing as soon as there is any submission to the outside rein. The reins should not be used to pull the head down, as this blocks the engagement of the hind quarters and creates resistance.

24. *A horse going above the bit.*

25. A horse dropping behind the bit.

If the horse is behind the bit (Fig. 25) he does not accept the rein contact, the front of the face is behind the vertical, and the poll is no longer the highest point of the neck. This can be due to the rider's hands being too strong, or his legs and seat too weak to drive the horse up to the hand, or the horse being asked to collect without enough impulsion. Other causes may be bad preliminary training, inconsistent contact on the reins, problems with sharp or wolf teeth. After the teeth have been checked it is corrected by riding the horse forward to a positive contact and with a forward feeling in the reins.

During training, many horses will drop behind the vertical. This is not a serious fault as long as the horse has lowered his head and is not trying to avoid the contact but is maintaining a light, elastic, consistent feel with the hand. The tendency does, however, become serious if it is allowed to persist for a long period.

If the horse is overbent the highest point of the neck is no longer the poll, and the front of the face is behind the vertical, but in this case the horse takes too much contact and brings his chin in towards his chest. Through bad training he may have learnt to pull, possibly due to too strong and unyielding hands. The horse must be encouraged to take the hand forwards and may need to be worked on a much lighter contact.

SUBMISSION

The rider gradually increases his control over the horse to make him mentally willing and physically capable of obedience. The aim is a horse 'on the aids', i.e. accepting the aids in a relaxed manner and submitting without resistance to the will of the rider. Submission does not mean a reluctant subservience but the establishment of harmony between horse and rider.

The horse should learn to accept the aids from the legs without tension, the seat of the rider without stiffening, and from the reins without resistance. For these aids to be effective and their co-ordination possible they must go 'through' the horse: i.e., the horse's hind quarters, back, neck and mouth are co-ordinated and connected by an elastic-like circuit so that the aids applied in any one of the areas will be felt in all the others. If this firm, elastic connection is blocked at any point by stiffness, tension, or resistance (i.e., is not submissive throughout the body), the aids will not go 'through' and cannot be harmoniously combined. Also the horse's movement will be short of his best and any collection will tend to be a slowing down rather than a shortening and heightening of the steps.

To develop submission. To achieve mental submission the rider has to establish a rapport with his horse, and be able to communicate with him. To do this he must:

□ Understand his horse – analyse his character, become aware of his physical strengths and weaknesses.

□ Give the horse the best opportunity to understand: i.e. be able to ask clearly, to apply the aids effectively. To achieve this end, Chapters 3 and 4 should be thoroughly studied.

To arrive at physical submission the horse must develop impulsion, rhythm (and balance), suppleness, straightness and acceptance of the bit, so that he will find it easy to work 'with' and not 'for' his rider.

IMPROVEMENT OF THE GAITS

The gaits should improve as the above objectives are developed. It is important for the rider to have a clear idea of what is correct (Chapter 5). He can then prevent faults occurring, correct any which have occurred, and aim to improve the natural gaits. At the trot and canter one of the aims must be to make the gaits more cadenced: i.e., to develop a pronounced rhythm, with energy to give more bounce to the strides through greater flexion of the joints and engagement of the hind quarters.

SUMMARY

The above objectives should be borne in mind throughout the basic training of the horse. They should be the end products of work divided into two stages (1) preparatory and (2) intermediate.

1. PREPARATORY STAGE

This stage of training (lasting four to twelve months, depending on the ability of the horse and trainer) aims to produce a horse which:
☐ Has fine, regular and unhurried gaits.
☐ Is calm, relaxed and obedient to the aids of the rider.
☐ Shows a good natural outline, balance and rhythm.
☐ Moves freely forward, without collection, but with active hind quarters.
☐ Accepts the bit willingly, without tension or resistance.
☐ Remains straight when moving on straight lines and bent when moving on curved lines.
☐ Executes transitions smoothly and remains still when halted.
☐ Is a pleasure to ride in the school and out of doors.

THE WORK

This should include:
☐ Work on the flat.
☐ Gymnastic jumping exercises.
☐ Riding out, including hill work.

WORK ON THE FLAT

Pattern of work. It is best to start at the rising trot on the horse's easiest rein and then to change to the more difficult rein. The first part of the work is aimed at loosening up and relaxing the horse by working him down.

All the work should be on both reins, and approximately equal time should be spent on each rein.

Frequent rest periods at the walk on a long rein are needed, and it is wise to finish on a good note performing a movement that the horse can do well.

When the horse trots with lively steps and a relaxed swinging back he should begin to present a degree of roundness in his outline, with the poll at the highest point of his neck. When he has reached this stage he is ready for the sitting trot.

Duration. Half an hour to fifty minutes, or two sessions of thirty minutes are average sessions, but it depends greatly on the strength and temperament of the individual horse.

THE FIGURES

From this early stage of training it is important to get into the discipline of executing accurate figures. The circles should be round, the straight lines straight, and the horse taken as deep into the corners as is possible without losing impulsion, rhythm, correct bend and the willingness to go forward. The circles should be limited to 20 metres (22 yds) in diameter, the half circles of 15 metres (50 ft) in diameter and the loops of a serpentine to a 12 metres (40 ft) diameter.

THE GAITS

These should be limited to a free walk on a long rein, the medium walk, a working trot and working canter. (See Chapter 5.)

When the horse is ready to canter he must learn to strike off on the correct leg. The easiest position for this is either when on a circle, or when going into the short side of the school. If he strikes off on the wrong leg he should not be made to halt – which he might regard as a form of punishment – but just to trot, and the strike off should be tried again. If for any reason the horse when asked to canter goes into a fast trot, he should not be allowed to strike off until a calm, relaxed working trot has been established.

Cantering is difficult for a young horse, especially on the circle, and should not be continued for too long. Many young horses find it easier to canter with their backs rounded and relaxed if the trainer is in a jumping position with his seat bones just out of the saddle.

THE TRANSITIONS

These should be progressive: i.e., not directly from canter to walk, but through trot, similarly with upward transitions. In the early stages of training, the manner in which a transition is executed is more important than its achievement at a given marker.

Transitions should be carried out smoothly but not abruptly. If the horse does not respond, ask again and again if necessary, so that the aids are repetitive, not continuous. For a transition to be satisfactory, the horse must be balanced as he goes into it, and must have sufficient impulsion. The rhythm of the gait should be maintained up to the moment that the gait is changed, or the horse is halted, and should be established in the new gait as soon as possible.

• *Upward transitions* (page 37). It is vital for the rider to prepare the young horse for an upward transition and, in particular, to develop enough impulsion to enable the horse to obey without throwing his head in the air or hollowing his back.

• *Downward transitions* (page 38). These must be *ridden* into, the trainer maintaining his correct seat and using a restraining but allowing hand. If he pulls backwards on the reins he will create resistances and stiffen the horse's back. In the early stages it is helpful to use the voice to avoid having to pull on the reins.

MOVEMENTS

These should be limited to the halt, the turn on the forehand, and an understanding of the half-halt.

THE HALF-HALT (page 39)

This is a hardly visible moderated version of the halt, which:
(a) Increases the attention and balance of the horse.
(b) Helps to engage the hind quarters, to generate impulsion, and to lighten the forehand.
(c) Warns the horse that the rider is about to ask something of him.
To be effective, the rider must, as in all the work, get the horse to think forward: i.e., the driving aids are more important than restraining aids. The seat and leg aids are applied to produce more activity in the hind quarters, which should have repercussions on other muscles in the horse's body (i.e., the muscles are co-ordinated, so the aids go 'through' and are not isolated to the hind quarters). To stop the driving aids simply increasing the horse's speed, the rein or reins momentarily restrain. This results in the increased energy and attention produced by the driving aids being contained within the horse, to result in a, b, and c above.

If the half-halt is to be effective, the back must be relaxed and swinging to enable the aids to go 'through' and allow the back to perform its function of acting as a connecting link between the forehand and the hind quarters. If the back is tense, the rein aids cannot go 'through' and the tendency will be for the horse to raise his head, hollow his back and lose the engaging effect of the half-halt.

After applying the rein aid the rider then gives momentarily with the hands so that the horse learns to hold himself together and does not rely for support on the reins. At the Intermediate stage the rider should aim to hold his horse with his seat and leg aids without reliance on the reins.

The half-halt becomes more important as training progresses, but the young horse should be gradually introduced to the aids and should learn to accept them correctly.

THE HALT (page 39)

It is important from the beginning of the ridden work, for the novice horse to be taught to stand still when halted. Initially he should be halted largely through use of the voice and with a light contact on the bit; for a second or two he should not move his legs or head. The novice horse should not be asked to stand still for too long; about three seconds is enough.

Too much importance should not be attached to the novice horse standing square. One hind leg is often left behind a little and it is better for the rider himself to remain still, rather than trying to correct the fault, which usually disappears as the horse becomes more supple. Not until the horse readily accepts the bit and is really going forward will he be able to bring his hind legs sufficiently under him to establish his balance and to stand with his weight equally adjusted over all four legs.

TURN ON THE FOREHAND (page 41)

In this movement the horse's hind quarters rotate around the forehand. The bend is normally away from the direction of the movement, but can be in the direction of the movement (Figs. 8 and 28G). It is the easiest movement to use for teaching the horse obedience to the lateral aids and can, therefore, be introduced at an early stage. It also helps to make the back supple.

AIMS

□ To teach the horse obedience to the leg aid.

□ To step neither backwards nor forwards.

□ Forelegs to move in a very small circle.

□ To bring the inside hind leg forward and under the horse.

EXECUTION

From the halt, to move the quarters to the right use the left leg close to the girth, and ask for a slight bend with the left leg, making sure that the right rein controls the forward movement and prevent the horse from bending his neck too much.

GYMNASTIC JUMPING EXERCISES

These are discussed in detail in Chapter 10.

As soon as the horse has learned to accept the bit, and to walk, trot, and canter without excitement, he should receive elementary jumping lessons. They are valuable in teaching the horse to use himself athletically, thereby strengthening his muscles and making him both supple and mentally alert. They can be given about twice a week, on good going. At this novice stage the jumps should be used to give a horse confidence and should never be too large. Work up from little fences to about 1 metre (3ft 6 in.) in height, with a maximum of 1.5 metres (5 ft) spread. Grids with accurately measured distances between the obstacles are initially the most valuable.

RIDING OUT

It is vital to keep a young horse's interest. He will soon tire of school work if he is weak and finds it an effort. Riding out, especially hill work, will help to develop his muscles as well as providing him with the variety which will be mentally refreshing.

Frequent riding out is, therefore, advisable, but the objects of training can still be kept in mind. Hacking across fields, over undulating ground, along lanes, need not be time off but another opportunity to develop the objectives of basic training.

In this outside work control is vital. If it is lost the horse and rider will be frightened, so a trainer must gauge how much can be asked of his pupil. He should not ask a nervous horse to go through heavy traffic or a busy town without the company of another more reliable horse. If going for a canter he should sense when the horse is showing signs of 'coming to the boil', and ease the pace before he loses control; then the occasional gallop can be enjoyed with safety.

Visits to horse shows, where a young horse can get used to crowds, other horses and strange sights, are a useful experience.

Towards the end of this stage of training, a day or two out with the local hunt can be beneficial, especially for potential eventers or jumpers who need to get accustomed to different obstacles, and for lazy horses to develop impulsion.

After riding out, the trainer should examine his horse in the stable for possible damage and in order to assess his general condition.

2. THE INTERMEDIATE STAGE

The intermediate stage is a continuation of the preparatory stage, further developing the objectives of training but with increasing emphasis being placed on collection.

COLLECTION

Collection (page 55) becomes an important objective at this stage, but it is only possible to develop if the trainer maintains and improves the other objectives: of impulsion, rhythm, suppleness, straightness, acceptance of the bit, submission and good gaits.

BENEFITS OF COLLECTION

□ The development and improvement of the horse's balance.

□ The engagement and lowering of his hind quarters, which will lighten and make his forehand more mobile. This enables the strides to become longer or higher, as desired.

□ The horse will develop more ease and self carriage in his work which will make him more pleasant to ride.

The horse should become more manoeuvrable, more able to generate the power to extend his gaits, carry out dressage movements, and jump fences.

TO COLLECT

Collection is achieved by greater engagement of the hind quarters, and not a slowing down to produce trudging, inactive steps. When asking the horse to shorten and heighten his strides into collection, impulsion must be maintained, or even increased.

The major aids for collection are half-halts, increasingly small circles, serpentines, variations within a gait, smooth direct downward and upward transitions and lateral movements.

WORK

This should include:
□ Work on the flat.
□ Gymnastic jumping exercises.
□ Riding out, including hill work and some strong canters on good going.
□ Competitions. If possible, occasional participation in such competitions as a one-day event of the type organised by the Riding Clubs, or Novice and Elementary dressage tests, or Novice show jumping. These would enable independent assessments of progress to be made.

WORK ON THE FLAT

The work first entails lengthening and loosening up the muscles, then flexing them into collection. When asking the horse for an effort, the trainer must first be certain of his aims and also that the horse is physically and mentally ready for the co-operation needed. If problems arise, revert to the basic principle of 'straighten your horse and ride him forward', as so many difficulties arise from loss of impulsion and crookedness.

The work must continue to be progressive, using the figures and movements shown below to improve the objectives of training. Thus from merely learning to remain immobile the horse can be taught to halt square and rein back; from the easiest lateral work of the turn on the forehand and leg yielding progress to the shoulder-in and half-pass; and from canter work at the counter-canter and use of simple changes progress to flying changes.

Not only should the movements tackled be progressive but also the manner in which they are performed. Thus the trainer will progress from achieving just a few steps of a movement to quite lengthy phases of the movement; from performing, for example, shoulder-in with little collection finishing on a circle, to shoulder-in down the length of the school in greater collection, finishing with the horse being straightened back on the track; from riding half-pass with very little bend and very much forward, to asking for a good deal of bend and sideways movement. Although trainers should keep in mind how Grand Prix horses perform movements, they must realise that it takes considerable muscular power and suppleness to perform them this way. They can only be developed with progressive work. Also, few eventers or show jumpers would be able, or need, to develop the collection needed for accurate Grand Prix dressage movements.

THE FIGURES

The trainer can gradually reduce the sizes of the circles as more collection is achieved to 10 metres (33 ft) diameter, and half circles of 6 metres (20 ft) diameter. The circles for the medium trot and medium canter should not be smaller than 20 metres (22 yds) diameter, and the extended canter should be ridden along straight tracks.

Serpentines are an excellent suppling exercise, especially if pear-shaped (as in Fig. 26). The size of the loops can be gradually reduced. The serpentine can be used in trot, and in canter with simple changes on the centre line, or some counter-canter loops.

(For other useful movements see Figs 27 and 28, pages 92-93.)

THE TRANSITIONS

As long as they are performed correctly, frequent transitions from one gait to another, and transitions within the gait, help to achieve the objectives of training.

When working, the trainer can gradually increase the degree of collection in his horse and can alternate this successively with the medium and extended gaits.

Transitions of two levels up: e.g., halt to trot, walk to canter, can be executed together with similar downward transitions.

The transitions should be made more quickly and less progressively than in the preliminary stage.

26. Diagram of a serpentine and a 15-metre half circle; exercises which are useful for the novice horse.

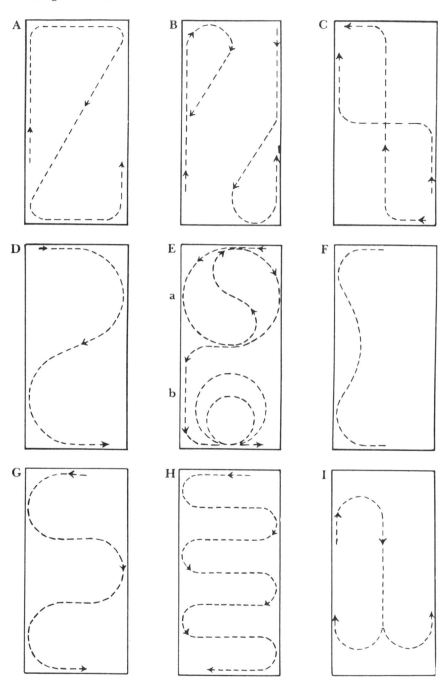

27. *Figures used during flatwork. A-D Methods of changing the rein. E (a) Change of rein within a 20-metre circle; (b) 15- and 10-metre circles. F Shallow loop. G. Three-loop serpentine. H. Six-loop serpentine. I. 10-metre half circles.*

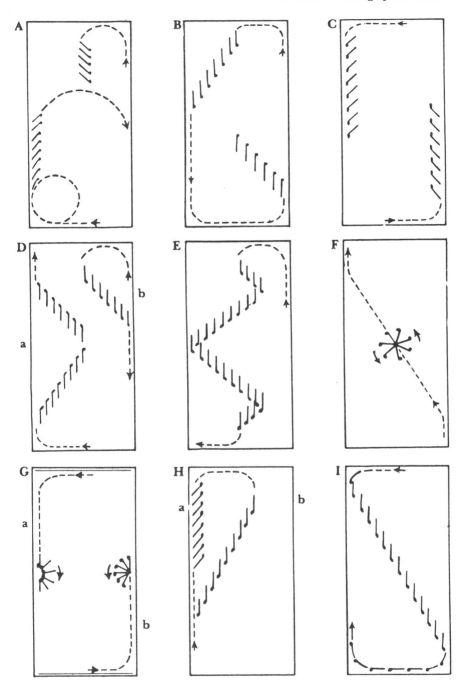

28. Diagram of figures incorporating lateral work. **A.** *Shoulder-in.* **B.** *Leg yielding.* **C.** *Renvers and travers.* **D. E. I.** *Half-pass.* **F.** *Pirouette.* **Ga.** *Turn on the forehand.* **Gb.** *Half pirouette.* **H.** *Renvers and half-pass.*

AIMS
- ☐ To show a clear transition.
- ☐ To be quick, but smooth and not abrupt.
- ☐ To maintain the rhythm of the gait up to the moment that the gait is changed, or the horse halts.
- ☐ For the new gait to be true and to show lively impulsion.
- ☐ For the horse to remain 'on the bit', light in hand, and calm.
- ☐ To remain balanced and on the bit.

THE HALT (page 39)

AIMS

At the halt in the preliminary stage the horse was first and foremost immobile, but not necessarily four square. Now the aims should be:
- ☐ To distribute the weight evenly on all four legs which are pairs abreast of each other (a square halt).
- ☐ To hold the neck so that the poll is the highest point and the head is slightly in front of the vertical.
- ☐ To remain 'on the bit' and maintain a supple jaw.
- ☐ To remain motionless, but attentive, and ready to move off at the wish of the rider.

EXECUTION

More of the horse's weight has to be transferred to his hind quarters by increasing the action of the rider's seat and legs, which should drive the horse towards a more and more restraining but allowing hand. By this intermediate stage the halt should be almost instantaneous, but not abrupt.

THE REIN-BACK (page 39)

The horse moves backwards, raising and setting down his legs in almost simultaneous diagonal pairs.

AIMS
- ☐ To lift the feet off the ground so that the limbs are not dragged.
- ☐ To remain straight.
- ☐ To step back in a deliberate rhythm.
- ☐ To make all the steps the same length.
- ☐ To move forward without halting when asked.

EXECUTION

The rein-back should not be asked for before the horse has become reasonably supple, flexible in his joints, and off his forehand, otherwise he will find it difficult and will have to be pulled back, which usually leads to a hollowing of the back and further resistances. If the horse does not respond in spite of being ready to learn to rein back, the rider must not pull him back, but should push him on to a stronger contact.

THE STAGES

□ Practise frequent smooth transitions to the halt, with the horse standing four square and remaining on the bit.

□ After a further good halt, apply the aids to move forward but with the hands restraining the forward movement. As the horse steps back, lighten the contact as a reward, but still keep him on the bit.

□ One or two steps are sufficient in the early stages.

□ After stepping back, the horse should walk forward without hesitation when asked to do so.

□ The rider must control each backward step and vary the number for which he asks.

THE COUNTER-CANTER (page 44)

The rider asks the horse to lead with the outside instead of the inside foreleg, so that when on a curve to the left the horse canters with the right lead.

AIMS

(a) To maintain the bend to the leading leg so that the horse looks to the outside of the curve.

(b) To keep the hind quarters from swinging to the outside of the curve.

(c) To maintain the rhythm and balance.

EXECUTION

The rider should only ask according to the suppleness and collection of his horse and should always bear in mind that the conformation of the horse does not allow him to be bent to the line of the circle. The early lessons can consist of loops off a straight line. Then progress as (a), (b), and (c) are maintained to circles and serpentines.

BENEFITS

□ An important suppling and balancing exercise.

□ Encourages the engagement of the hind quarters if carried out correctly.

□ Can be of use when teaching the flying changes.

THE SIMPLE CHANGE OF LEG (page 44)

The leading leg at the canter is changed by making a downward transition to walk, and after two or three walk strides the canter is re-established with the other leg leading.

AIMS

□ To execute the movement smoothly.

□ To remain on the bit.

□ To maintain impulsion.

□ To keep the hind quarters engaged.
□ To remain straight.

THE FLYING CHANGE OF LEG (page 44)

This takes place during a period of suspension in the canter when both fore and hind legs should change together, the leading hind leg initiating the change.

AIMS

□ To remain light, calm and straight.
□ To maintain impulsion.
□ To maintain the same rhythm and balance.
□ To achieve a noticeable and clean jump from one leading leg to the other (i.e. the change has expression).

The flying change should not be attempted before:

□ The horse's hind quarters are strong.
□ The horse has the ability to collect at the canter and to maintain impulsion.
□ The horse is balanced and straight.
□ The horse remains 'on the bit' during his work.
□ The canter strike-offs are correct.

PREPARATION

He should be made to do simple changes at short intervals on alternate legs. When these are well performed with a degree of collection, the horse remaining straight and 'on the aids', the trainer should ask for alternately true and counter-canter through the walk.

EXECUTION

To make the first flying change as easy as possible for the horse, he is usually cantered across the school on a diagonal in a well-balanced, well-collected canter, and asked to change at the end of the diagonal. If the change has been correctly made, the horse should first be settled before being rewarded with a walk on a long rein. If the change was not correct or not made at all, the rider might try once more and, if again it is a failure, he should return to the preparatory exercises before retrying. It is essential that the change should not be late behind: i.e., the change is made first with the forelegs and then a stride or more later with the hind legs. Unless the rider can feel such an error from the saddle, he should have an assistant on the ground to tell him whether the change has been correctly performed.

ALTERNATIVE SITUATIONS IN WHICH TO ASK FOR A CHANGE

Although most trainers teach their horses flying changes at the end of a diagonal, some horses find the following positions easier. If the horse does not change correctly at the end of the diagonal, these positions can be tried. Also, when continuing the training it is vital to ensure that a horse does not anticipate and start to change of his own accord. Therefore, ask for the change from different positions.

THE ALTERNATIVES

□ From the counter-canter, which can be executed down the long side of the school. To prevent anticipation the rider should sometimes continue in the counter-canter beyond the points where he usually asks for a change. It is most important for the horse to remain straight throughout the movement and to avoid any sideways drift. It is important, too, for the horse to change on the aids and not to anticipate.

□ From the canter half-pass allow one or two straight strides then ask for the change.

□ In a serpentine ask for the change when crossing the centre line.

□ From a 10 or 15 metre (33 or 50 ft) half circle ask for the change when just about to return to the track.

LATERAL WORK

In lateral work the horse moves sideways as well as forwards. This helps to:

□ Increase the obedience of the horse.

□ Supple the horse, increasing the freedom of the shoulders, mobility of the hind quarters and the elasticity of that vital bond connecting the hind quarters, back, neck, poll and the mouth.

□ To improve the cadence and balance.

□ To help engage the hind quarters and so increase collection.

AIMS

□ Gaits to remain free and regular.

□ To maintain impulsion, rhythm and balance.

□ To achieve a slight bend from the poll to the tail (except leg yielding when the horse is only bent at the poll). The amount of bend depends on the suppleness and stage of training of the horse. It must never be so excessive (i.e. rider preoccupied with going sideways) that fluency, balance and impulsion are inhibited.

LEG YIELDING (page 42)

In the leg yield the horse moves forward and sideways. He should be straight, except for a slight bend at the poll, allowing the rider to see the eyebrow and nostril on the inside. This bend is in the opposite direction to that in which he is moving. The inside legs pass and cross the outside legs.

It is the easiest of the lateral movements, requiring no collection, and is therefore especially valuable in the training of young horses. It is used by many trainers as a means of introducing lateral work. It is a movement which has caused controversy, and not all trainers are in agreement about its use. (Figs 8b and 28B)

97

EXECUTION

The first lessons are best given at the walk. Only when the horse under-stands the aids should it be tried at the trot. The usual figures for trying the leg yield are:

□ From a 10 metres (33 ft) circle leg yield out to either the long side of the arena or to start a 20 metre (22 yd) circle.

□ From the short side of the arena turn down the centre line and leg yield to the long side.

□ Along the diagonal when the horse should be as close as possible parallel to the long side but with the forehand just in advance.

□ Along the wall when the horse should not be at a greater angle than 35° to the direction in which he is moving.

SHOULDER-IN (page 42)

In the shoulder-in the horse moves at an angle of about 30° to the direction of the movement, with his whole body bent slightly, around the rider's inside leg, while looking away from the direction in which he is moving. The horse's inside foreleg passes and crosses in front of the outside leg; the inside hind leg is placed in front of the outside leg. It can be executed on straight lines or circles. (Figs 8c and 28A)

BENEFITS

The shoulder-in is the foundation of all collected and advanced lateral work. Because of this, it is perhaps the most valuable of all exercises available to the trainer:

□ It is suppling and collecting movement, as the inside hind leg is brought well under the body and placed in front of the outside. To do this the horse must lower his inside hip and flex the joints of the hind leg.

□ It helps the rider to control the shoulder of the horse. By 'thinking shoulder-in' when riding turns and circles, and particularly before striking off to canter, it helps to prevent the shoulder falling out or the quarters coming in.

□ It helps to make the horse straight.

□ It improves the quality of the gaits.

□ It can be used to discipline a horse.

AIMS

□ To maintain impulsion and willingness to go forward.

□ To maintain rhythm.

□ The bend should be through the body and not just the neck, otherwise the collecting value is lost and the shoulders tend to fall out.

□ The hind quarters should not swing out (that is quarters-out instead of shoulder-in).

□ The movement itself should go 'through' the horse: that is the elastic bond between the hind quarters and mouth maintained at all times.

EXECUTION

Sometimes a first lesson is given at the walk, but as soon as the horse understands what is wanted, the movement should be executed at the trot. The usual way to begin the movement is on completion of a corner before the long side of the school. Instead of riding down the long side the rider continues on the curve of the corner, bringing the forehand away from the track but keeping the hind legs still on the track, where they should remain throughout the movement. The rider when guiding the forehand off the track increases the pressure from his inside leg and the restraining action of the outside rein, while maintaining the bend with the inside rein and controlling the hind quarters with the outside leg.

At first, only a few steps of shoulder-in should be asked for, followed by the horse being ridden forward on a single track in the direction he was facing. The number of steps can be increased as performance and suppleness improve.

THE TRAVERS AND RENVERS (page 43)

In the travers (quarters-in) and the renvers (quarters-out) (Figs 8d, 8e and 28C), the horse is slightly bent around the inside leg of the rider and positioned at an angle of about 30° to the line of the track. They differ from the shoulder-in in that the horse looks in the direction in which he is moving. They can be performed along the wall or centre line.

BENEFITS
□ To increase obedience.
□ To prepare for the half-pass.
□ To increase the control over the hind quarters.
□ As a collecting exercise in the canter they can be used in the preparation for the pirouette.

EXECUTION
The early lessons are usually given in the walk, but can later be carried out at trot and canter. To execute travers: at the end of the short side, instead of straightening on to the track, the bend of the turn is maintained and the aids for travers are applied.

As the renvers is an inverted travers it uses the same muscles, etc., as the travers.

THE HALF-PASS (page 43)

This is a variation of travers, executed on the diagonal. (Figs 8f and 28D, E and I.) The horse is slightly bent around the inside leg of the rider and should be aligned as nearly as possible parallel to the long side of the school, but with the forehand slightly in advance of the hind quarters. At trot and walk the outside legs cross and pass in front of the inside legs, but at the canter it is usual for the legs not to cross. The horse looks forward and sideways in the direction in which he is moving.

AIMS

□ To maintain the same balance and rhythm throughout the entire movement.

□ To maintain a bend, but this must not be so excessive that it leads to a loss of impulsion.

□ To ensure the forehand is light so that there is freedom and mobility in the shoulders and ease and grace to the movement.

EXECUTION

Correct execution depends greatly on how the horse goes into the movement and how well the forward element predominates. The trainer might begin the lesson with a half-volte followed by the half-pass (Fig. 28Db). A useful alternative is shoulder-in along the short side and, as the corner is turned, half-pass across the diagonal; or to leg yield from the centre line to the long side and return to the centre line in half-pass.

HALF-PIROUETTE AT THE WALK (page 43)

This is a half circle performed on two tracks with a radius equal to the length of the horse. The forehand moves around the haunches. The fore feet and the outside hind foot move around the inside hind foot, which acts as the pivot, returning to the same spot or just in front of it each time it is lifted.

AIMS

□ The horse should be slightly bent to the direction in which he is moving.

□ To remain on the bit.

□ To maintain the rhythm of the walk.

□ The horse should not move backwards.

EXECUTION

The horse can be taught to respond to the aids for the walk pirouette by at first asking him for travers on a small circle. As he manages to retain the impulsion and sequence of the walk footfalls the size of the circle can be reduced until it becomes a walk pirouette (Fig. 28Gb).

INTRODUCTION OF THE DOUBLE BRIDLE

The double bridle puts finishing touches, or the final polish, on movements which have already been taught and well executed when ridden in a snaffle. It can be worn after the horse has been introduced to lateral work and is accepting the bit in all work. Its first introduction should be with some simple work on a single track. Variations of pace within a gait will help to establish good impulsion and will encourage the trainer to ride the horse on to the bit.

The frequency of the use of the double bridle depends upon the rider and the horse.

SUMMARY

When the horse is able to perform well all the school movements of the Intermediate stage he should be a very good ride. It is a level of training which would benefit show jumpers; advanced event horses have to be able to do the work (except flying changes) in order to perform the FEI Three-Day-Event Test. More advanced training on the flat is not important for show jumpers or eventers, so the next chapter is usually treated as the sphere of the specialist dressage horse.

9 Advanced Training on the Flat

INTRODUCTION

At this stage the rider/horse partnership begins to specialise. If dressage is chosen, ultimately 'The dressage rider is an artist and the horse is his medium; together they produce a work of art' (Hans Handler). Only the great riders and horses can achieve this, but it should still be the aim of everybody embarking on this advanced training.

The more particular aims at this stage should be to train the horse to be:
□ Responsive to delicate aids.
□ Exceptionally supple in all gaits and movements.
□ Able to generate great impulsion and collection.

To achieve these aims the rider must become:
□ An analyst who pays great attention to detail and is quick to recognise faults and problems.
□ Open minded – ready to admit an error, eager to learn and, if necessary, willing to adjust his means of achieving the ends.
□ Dedicated and able to work with enthusiasm day after day.
□ Aware that no horse can perfect his movements unless he is skilfully ridden. The rider's balance, posture and correct application of aids become critical and can only be developed and maintained through great determination and discipline.

FACILITIES

At this stage, regular work is vital. It should be on good going, as hard, rough ground jars the horse and stiffens his back. It is also important to have enough space to develop the extensions. Therefore, either a large indoor school or outdoor arena 20 metres (22 yds) x 60 metres (66 yds) becomes a practical necessity.

ASSISTANCE

Help from a knowledgeable person on the ground is vital, not necessarily every day, but regularly, to check the rider's position and the horse's paces and movements.

HORSEMASTERSHIP

Attention to detail includes the care of the horse, who needs:
□ To be well fed as he must be very fit to do advanced work.
□ Consistent grooming to keep him clean and to tone up his muscles.
□ Constant attention to his physical well-being as strains, sores, etc., if not put right, will affect his work.

OBJECTIVES OF TRAINING

The objectives remain the same as in the previous chapter, pages 76 to 84, though some should be nearer to achieving success than others. Thus, by this stage the horse should be submissive, straight, accepting the bit and able to establish a rhythm. The major area for improvement will be:
□ Suppleness (page 78)
□ Impulsion (page 77)
□ Collection (pages 55 and 89).

GENERAL SCHOOL WORK

With the possible exception of the turn on the forehand, all the exercises of the Intermediate stage can be included in this basic school work.

The gaits
More time can be spent on the walk to develop the variations within this basic gait. The collected and extended walk must be developed, but with great care. An assistant on the ground should check that the sequence of footfalls remains true, for the rhythm is all too easily lost with so little impulsion being produced at the walk.

Greater variations within the trot and canter should be asked for, but taking care to develop enough impulsion to make this possible without hurrying in the extensions, or slowing down in the collections.

Circles
Ridden at the collected trot and canter can be gradually reduced in size from 10 metres (33 ft) diameter to 6 metres (20 ft) diameter (a volte).
AIMS
□ The hind quarters should not swing inwards or outwards.
□ To avoid excessive bend in the neck.
□ Horse and rider should not lean in (or out).

□ Rhythm is maintained during and when entering and leaving the circles.

□ To perform circles equally well on both reins.

Serpentines

These should by now be relatively easy suppling exercises at the collected or working trot, and useful variations can be used at the canter. Loops can be performed at the counter-canter as well as at the true canter, and the width of the loops can be reduced as the horse becomes more collected, so that the exercise becomes progressively more difficult: i.e., use a four-loop serpentine in a 20-metre (22 yd) × 60-metre (66 yd) arena at first and then progress to six loops. Flying changes can be executed on the centre line of the serpentine; however, simple changes are also a most useful suppling exercise.

AIMS

□ The loops to be of a similar size and shape.

□ Simple or flying changes to be executed fluently and accurately.

□ Rhythm to be maintained.

□ Correct bend to be maintained.

Transitions

The following direct transitions can be practised:

UPWARD TRANSITIONS

□ Halt to collected trot.

□ Rein back to collected trot or canter.

□ Collected walk to collected canter.

□ Halt to collected canter.

Later:

□ Piaffe to collected trot.

□ Piaffe to passage.

DOWNWARD TRANSITIONS

□ Extension to collection at all three gaits.

□ Collected walk, collected canter, and collected and medium trot to halt.

Later:

□ Passage or piaffe to halt.

AIMS – As on page 86.

LATERAL WORK

The half-pass, travers and renvers should be executed with a greater degree of collection and sideways movement, but only insofar as the essential impulsion and fluency are maintained.

The counter change of hand (zigzag) is a series of half-passes either side of a line (Fig. 28E).

TO EXECUTE AT THE TROT

From a half-pass to the right the rider's outside (left) leg is used to direct the hind quarters slightly further over to the right and at the same time the horse's bend is changed so that the forehand can take the lead. The aids are then applied for a half-pass to the left.

TO EXECUTE AT THE CANTER

From a half-pass to the right the rider stops driving the horse laterally and rides him straight forward for two or three strides, during which time he asks for the change and the new bend to the left before applying the aids for the half-pass left. When the horse can perform the change fluently and equally well from right to left half-pass or vice versa, the number of straight strides can be reduced to ultimately one, when the new bend is asked for during the change.

AIMS

□ The forehand must always lead in the half-pass.

□ The horse must take strides of equal length in both directions of the half-pass.

□ Impulsion, rhythm and balance must be maintained throughout the movement.

FLYING CHANGES (page 44)

When the horse can execute single flying changes 'on the aids' and in balance he should be ready to start a series of flying changes, which are executed regularly after a given number of strides. The number of strides between changes can be reduced as he masters the easier series from, say, five to two (two-time changes) and finally to changes every stride (one-time changes).

EXECUTION

In these series the degree of collection should be slightly less than in the collected canter to ensure a good forward bound at each change.

One particular series should not be practised for too long, as the horse then tends to anticipate and will not change on the aids. The series and the number of changes asked in any series should be varied.

If teaching a more difficult series, end the lesson on one that is easy for him: that is, four times after doing some two or one times.

AIMS

□ Keeping the horse straight. Any tendency to drift or swing should be corrected by:

(a) Guiding the forehand, thinking shoulder-in, as each change is asked for.

(b) Increasing the impulsion, riding forward into the changes at a stronger canter: using the inside leg to achieve this.

□ The change to be executed with the forelegs and hind legs changing simultaneously. If the change is late behind, this is usually due to either the horse being on his forehand or to the rider using too much rein and not enough leg. More impulsion and collection should be generated.

□ Rhythm and impulsion must be maintained. If the horse moves more and more slowly through the series he should be ridden forward and asked to change at a medium canter. If he moves more and more quickly, half-halts should be applied during the strides when he is not changing.

PIROUETTE AT THE CANTER (page 43)

The pirouette (half-pirouette) is a circle (half circle) performed on two tracks with a radius equal to the length of the horse. The forehand moves around the hind quarters, the forefeet and the outside hind foot moving around the inside hind foot which is lifted and put down again on the same spot, or slightly in front of it.

AIMS

□ To keep the horse 'on the bit' with a light contact and a slight bend to the direction in which he is turning.

□ To maintain balance, rhythm and impulsion.

□ To maintain the regularity of the canter hoof beats. The inside hind leg is lifted and returned to the ground in the same rhythm as the outside hind foot, and should not remain on the ground.

□ The strides should be accentuated, cadenced, and for a full pirouette should be six to eight in number and for a half-pirouette three to four.

EXECUTION

The pirouette at the canter is one of the most difficult of all the advanced movements, as it calls for a high degree of collection and great impulsion. Horses should only be taught pirouettes after they have developed a good collected canter full of impulsion, are responding correctly to the half-halt, and are able to shorten the canter so much that for a few strides they almost remain on the spot (still in three-time) before willingly going forward again.

VARIOUS METHODS

● *From a large-walk pirouette* and one in which the hind quarters are very well engaged, strike off into the canter while maintaining the same aids as for the walk pirouette. The horse should canter pirouette for a few steps before cantering straight forward (if he lacks impulsion) or returning to the walk (if he becomes excitable). The success of this method depends on the strike-off being of high quality.

● *From the renvers.* At the end of a long side the rider asks for a very small half circle (or passade) to canter in renvers parallel to the long side, and then turns towards the wall to perform a three-quarter pirouette. This method enables better control over the outside hind leg at the moment of starting the pirouette (one of the commonest faults is for the hind quarters to swing outwards). Also, the horse is already in the correct bend. (Fig. 29.)

29. Diagram of use of passade and renvers to perform a canter pirouette.

● *From a large circle.* This can be more difficult, as it is not so easy to prevent the hind quarters falling out, but is a useful progression after the above two methods towards a pirouette on a single track. Voltes are performed within the large circle, eventually making them so small they become a passade and finally, a half-pirouette. Then proceed in counter-canter before trying on the other rein.

● *From travers on a large circle,* or from half-pass.

● *From a straight line,* but this should not be tried until the horse performs a satisfactory pirouette in the above methods. The rider should give his horse a slight shoulder-in position when approaching the point to which the pirouette is to be carried out, and the canter highly collected so that he is almost cantering on the spot when he is asked to turn into the pirouette (Fig. 28F).

If during attempts at the pirouette, the horse moves into the walk, it is important to keep asking with the aids for the pirouette, but with more vigour so that he returns to the canter. If he starts to swing around quickly, to swivel on his inside hind leg, return to work at the travers or renvers so that control over every collected stride can be maintained. Also, he can be asked to walk during the pirouette, perform a few steps of the pirouette at walk and then strike off into the canter, still in the pirouette when more control over each stride should have been established.

It is vital during the pirouette for the rider to retain the correct position, to remain upright with his seat in the saddle and to avoid tipping forward or to the outside with the momentum of the movement.

When working on pirouettes it is important to remember that they are demanding of the horse and should not be attempted for too long. It is important, too, for the size of the pirouette to be varied from half to three-quarter to whole, so that the horse remains on the aids and ready to come out of it whenever asked.

THE PIAFFE (page 45)

This is a highly collected, elevated and cadenced trot on the spot.

AIMS

□ The height of the toe of the raised foreleg should be level with the middle of the cannon bone of the other foreleg. The toe of the raised hind leg should reach just above the fetlock joint of the other hind leg.

□ The neck should be raised and arched, the head perpendicular, the back supple and swinging, and the hind quarters slightly lowered, with active hocks well engaged to give great freedom, lightness and mobility to the shoulders and forehand.

□ Each diagonal pair of legs should be raised and returned to the ground alternately with an even rhythm and a definite, but short, period of suspension.

□ The piaffe should be produced as a result of great impulsion, so the horse should be ready and willing to move forward at all times.

□ The horse should not move backwards, cross the forelegs, swing the forehand, or hind quarters, or take irregular steps.

□ The horse should remain 'on the bit' with a supple poll and a light, but taut, rein.

EXECUTION

The piaffe can be taught either from the ground or from the saddle. In the former method it is easier for the horse to use his back without the weight of the rider, but some horses find the latter easier to understand.

Teaching from the ground. These lessons should take place in a closed arena and the stages are as follows:

1. The horse is brought to the middle of the arena, fitted with a snaffle, saddle, cavesson, lunge rein and side-reins. The side-reins should be adjusted so that they just make contact when the horse is collected. It may be necessary to shorten them as he becomes more collected. The lunge rein is attached to the cavesson and the horse is taken to the track on the left rein, as this is the easiest for most horses and convenient for the trainer.

2. The trainer positions himself near the shoulder of the horse. Taking up a fairly short rein in his left hand and holding the whip in his right hand he walks the horse slowly once or twice around the arena. As soon as the horse is walking in a calm and relaxed manner, he can be asked to trot. The hind legs should initiate this transition and the steps should be short. If the horse tries to go forward too much, the trainer should apply restraining aids with the hand. If the horse is reluctant to go forward, touch him with the whip just above the hind fetlocks. The voice should be used to supplement these driving and restraining aids. When the horse can work calmly and with rhythm in this exercise, the teaching of piaffe can begin.

3. With the horse standing correctly at halt on a long side of the arena, the trainer should position himself, as before, alongside the shoulder of his horse with his whip in his right hand. He will now take up a very short rein, holding his left hand closely behind the head of his horse. (Fig 30.) From the halt the horse should be asked to move forward with a few steps of very collected trot and then brought again to the halt; this time the trainer should move to stand directly in front of his horse. The horse will soon come to understand that the trainer at his side means activity, and that the

30. Teaching a horse piaffe from the ground.

trainer in front means immobility.

Eventually the aim must be for the horse to work on both reins, but for the first day the trainer may be satisfied with a few good steps on one rein. Over a series of lessons the trainers should progressively ask the horse to shorten the trot strides and should increase the collection. The hind legs must come further under the body; to encourage them to do so and to spring elastically off the ground, the trainer can use the whip to touch the hind legs. Only a few strides at a time should be asked for in this manner.

4. When seven or eight perfectly level steps can be executed without moving forward further than one yard, the horse may be ridden: but the rein should still be in the hands of the trainer, who continues to control the horse from the ground in the same manner as before. Eventually, the trainer can ride the horse to perfect the movement.

THE TRAINER'S MAIN CONSIDERATIONS SHOULD BE:

□ Never to ask too much. The horse has to work hard to produce the necessary impulsion and bouncy spring to his action, so the lessons should not last too long and should end if possible, on a good, calm note.

□ The horse must remain straight. If he tries to bring his hind quarters from the wall, the trainer should counter with a slight shoulder-in position.

□ The strides must be level. The trainer should never sacrifice levelness through efforts to produce more elevated steps.

□ The horse should always move forward – if only one inch per step – until training has reached its final stage, when 10 to 12 steps on the spot will be the aim.

□ The hind legs should not be brought too far under the body or the hind quarters will be over-burdened. The horse will then have difficulty in lifting his hind feet off the ground which tends to make the trot irregular and the forward transitions abrupt.

Teaching from the saddle. This method, although usually easier for the trainer (since he should have more control) makes it more difficult for the horse to use his back elastically.

The principle considerations and progressive training methods are similar to those outlined in training from the ground. An assistant trainer walks alongside the horse's hind quarters. The rider applies the aids for piaffe, and the assistant, if necessary, taps with the whip to encourage the horse to flex his hind legs and to place them further under his body. As soon as the horse steps correctly with diagonal pairs, the forelegs rising higher than the hind legs, he can be asked to carry out this work more energetically. To achieve this the collection has to be built up so that just before asking for piaffe-like steps, walk pirouettes and transitions from a shortened trot to halt (and vice versa) can be performed.

It is advisable to teach piaffe first, but if the horse is naturally short of impulsion, the passage may be taught before the piaffe, not only to improve the impulsion but to teach the horse to spring energetically off the ground.

PASSAGE (page 45)

This is a very collected, very elevated and very cadenced trot. Each diagonal pair of feet is raised higher and with a longer period of suspension than for any other trot.

AIMS

☐ The toe of the raised foreleg should be level with the middle of the cannon bone of the other foreleg. The toe of the raised hind leg should be slightly above the fetlock joint of the other hind leg: i.e., as in piaffe.

☐ The neck should be raised and arched, with the poll as the highest point and the head close to the perpendicular. The horse should remain on the bit, accepting a light contact.

☐ The hind quarters should be well engaged and the flexion of the knees and hocks should be accentuated, but with graceful elasticity of movement.

☐ The impulsion should be lively and pronounced and the horse should be able to go smoothly from the passage to the piaffe, and vice versa, without apparent effort and without altering the rhythm.

☐ The steps should be regular and neither the forehand nor the hind quarters should swing from one side to the other.

EXECUTION

The passage is taught usually from the saddle. It is developed out of the piaffe, the collected trot, or sometimes the walk, depending on the abilities and temperament of the horse. It is most usual to teach from the piaffe, as long as the horse has mastered this movement.

The horse is ready to be taught passage when he is capable of positive collection and extension, and of containing his impulsion.

An assistant on the ground may be useful, as he can come close to the hind quarters, with a long whip if necessary, and without upsetting the horse can indicate that more impulsion and elevation are required.

The rider applies his legs, the pressures being in the rhythm of the passage, and he sits deep, using the forward driving influence of his seat (page 31). The hands restrain, saying 'no faster', so that the increased impulsion goes upwards to produce passage – the elevated steps gaining little ground. When passage-like steps are achieved they should be maintained just long enough for the horse to understand that this is what is required and then given a reward.

The rider can reduce the pressure of his legs when the horse goes into passage and cease the pressure when he wants the horse to return to trot.

As with piaffe, regularity in all its aspects if of prime importance. Only when this can be achieved and maintained should the trainer strive for greater elevation.

The movement should be smooth and flowing, without jerky prop-like landings of the forelegs, or hollowing of the back.

Care must be taken that the long whip, used to stimulate activity by applying it to the hind-quarters, is not employed too much or too often, so that its stimulating effect is lost.

VARIATIONS OF PASSAGE

Each horse has his characteristic natural type of trot, which should appear in his piaffe and passage. This is why there is so much variation in the types of passage performed. Ideally, the speed of the rhythm (tempo) remains the same in piaffe and passage.

DRESSAGE COMPETITIONS

Most serious riders aim to compete in dressage competitions and to achieve success the following are important prerequisites:

□ To have a relaxed horse at the competitions. This usually entails frequent visits to shows, whether competing or not, especially with high-spirited, temperamental or young horses.

□ Careful organisation of the 'riding-in' period, taking into account the character and abilities of the horse and the test to be performed. The work to be included (lungeing, walking around, loosening up, etc.) and the time it will take should be planned beforehand.

□ Study of judges' sheets to ascertain the defects which need most attention and then training accordingly.

□ Development of 'arena craft' which entails careful study of the test to be performed, accurate execution of it, good use of the arena, and determination to show off the horse at his best.

10 Training the Horse to Jump

INTRODUCTION

Horses are born with varying degrees of jumping ability. The trainer's task is to develop the horse's ability, giving him the confidence to jump many different types of obstacles and to do so when carrying a rider.

TO JUMP

A horse jumping correctly from a balanced, calm, yet energetic approach to an obstacle appears to do so with ease. During the last few strides of the approach he stretches his head and neck forward and downwards, then raises them to spring upwards off his forehand. This takes place a moment before the hind feet meet the ground. The powerful muscles of the hind quarters and thighs, and the leverage of the hips, stifles, hocks and fetlocks, push the horse upwards and forwards over the obstacle.

During take-off and over the obstacle, the horse's back should be rounded, not hollow, with the withers as the highest point and with the head and neck stretched forward to help his balance (known as basculing; Fig. 23, page 79.)

On descent, the head and neck rise slightly and the forelegs meet the ground one after the other, followed by the hind legs.

This style is the most efficient method of jumping and demands least effort from the horse. But it takes time to build up the muscles and to develop the suppleness to enable him to jump in this way. Rushed training usually results in incorrect muscle development, less efficient styles (e.g., a hollow back in mid-air) and often eventually – because it takes an effort to jump – a loss of confidence and refusal.

The muscles which should be developed through flat work, riding out, especially up and down hills, and gymnastic jumping exercises, are as follows:
□ The upper neck muscles, *not* those on the underside.
□ The shoulder and forearm.
□ Back and loin, which are probably the most important.
□ Second thigh muscles.

THE TRAINING PROGRAMME

The work for at least the first year of the horse's ridden life is common to an eventer, a jumper and a dressage horse. He should be backed as described in Chapter 7, and trained on in the way described in Chapter 8, the Preparatory Stage.

The flat work is vital in order to develop the correct muscles and the controlled riding necessary to jump in the above style. In the case of the potential show jumper, greater emphasis can be placed on jumping in conjunction with this flat work. Easy obstacles should be used so that he gradually builds up his ability and confidence.

When he is being backed, and during the early riding days, he can be lunged over trotting poles and very small fences. If the facilities are available he could be loose-schooled. After he relaxes when ridden, and when he is sufficiently obedient and fit, the rider can take him over trotting poles, then progress gradually to small obstacles, with the size and variety of the jumps being slowly increased.

The rate of progress will depend upon the ability of the horse and rider, but the essential factors are:

□ The jumping should be fun for the horse, so he must not be asked too much for his stage of training, nor should he be asked to jump when tired. Schooling sessions over jumps should be short.

□ Slightly more difficult fences may be tackled when the horse can jump the easier obstacles in the styles described above, but if at any time he loses his confidence, return to the easier obstacles. It is important that in each jumping lesson he is loosened up over trotting poles and small fences; gradually progressing to ever larger obstacles.

LUNGEING OVER SMALL OBSTACLES

The horse first learns to jump without a rider on his back, on the lunge. Start by walking over a pole on the ground, progress to trotting over a series of poles and to jumping solid single obstacles. Remember at all times that it is difficult for the horse to jump off the turn and it takes great skill and experience on the part of the lunger to give him the necessary assistance. Therefore, for most trainers it is advisable to restrict the work on the lunge to trotting poles and single obstacles of not more than about 1 metre (3 ft). For techniques of lungeing over obstacles see pages 64-65.

LOOSE SCHOOLING OVER OBSTACLES

If the horse can be made to jump loose, calmly, rhythmically and with impulsion, he will learn to look after himself and to develop a good style of jumping. Damage can be done with inadequate facilities, and/or inexperienced trainers, resulting in the horse running out, refusing, or starting to rush his fences. Like lungeing, loose schooling is only of value if done well.

Requirements
☐ An indoor school or small enclosure from which it is impossible for the horse to escape, or a jumping lane consisting of a series of small fences.
☐ If an indoor school or enclosure is used, the obstacles should have wings to discourage the horse from running out.
☐ The horse should be obedient to aids of the voice and the lunge whip.

Techniques. The horse, wearing a head collar or cavesson and protective boots, should be led around the school once or twice and then let loose and sent round at the trot, driven on when necessary by his trainer's voice and lunge whip. An assistant is needed and should be responsible for driving the horse forward in one half of the school. The trainer and assistant should never be in front of the horse as he moves round the track.

When the horse trots calmly and willingly around the school, an obstacle with wings can be erected. It is advisable to place the poles on the ground, and only when the horse trots over them confidently should they be raised. The best position for the obstacle is usually soon after the corner. Placing poles (see page 117), of 2.60 to 3 metres (8 to 9½ ft), or 5.50 to 6 metres (17½ to 20 ft) in front of the jumps are advisable to stop the horse rushing, or arriving at an awkward take-off position. Alternatively, a pole can be placed diagonally in the corner and the small obstacle 16 metres (52 ft) away from it.

It is vital for the trainer and the assistant to present the horse straight at the fence and not to chase him into it. It is essential for the horse to jump of his own accord, encouraged by the voice and the presence of the whip.

Obstacles should never be 'trappy', nor too high. At a later stage multiple fences may be used.

The horse should be rewarded frequently during loose schooling sessions. After a few good circuits he should be stopped, patted, and occasionally given titbits.

JUMPING WITH A RIDER

The horse should be ready to jump with a rider only after he has learned to jump without a rider, has been backed, is fit and responsive to the aids.

GENERAL PRINCIPLES

☐ It is advisable when jumping to have an assistant present to put up obstacles, to ensure that the distances between fences are correct, and also for reasons of safety.

□ The obstacles should be solid or substantial so that the horse does not become careless through finding it easy to hit fences. At the same time, they should be 'inviting', to encourage him to jump and not to run out, and should be kept small enough to prevent him being over-faced.

□ Distances between the obstacles and the placing and trotting poles should be 'correct' until an advanced stage of training.

□ The young horse should be started over fences with which he is familiar and which he has jumped successfully on the lunge. When trying a strange obstacle it is advisable to make it small in height; to show it to him first; to let him sniff at it; and with nervous horses, to follow an experienced horse over the fence. At all costs, refusals should be avoided.

□ Jumping causes strain on a young horse's tendons and feet. Sprains and lameness can result, particularly if the ground is too hard, or too soft, or if the horse is not fit enough for the work demanded. Long jumping sessions should be avoided.

N.B. There is no need to jump massive fences at home. The aim of the trainer is to familiarise the horse with all types of obstacles and to develop a style which will make jumping as easy as possible. This can be achieved over low obstacles, and even advanced horses need not practise over more than 1.2 metre (4 ft) obstacles.

METHOD OF RIDING

The rider must be a competent horseman if he is to do this work without hindering his horse. Although remaining in control he should not try to 'place' the horse (adjusting his stride so that he takes off in a particular position).

After presenting his horse straight at the obstacle he should have the following aims in mind:

□ To sit as still as possible in the correct position.

□ To retain a light rein contact.

□ Although allowing the horse as far as possible to approach and jump the obstacles in his own way, sufficient impulsion is essential and at times the rider might have to generate this with his legs and – if necessary – with his seat and taps of the whip. (See page 77.)

□ The horse will find it easier to jump in the correct style if he approaches the fence in balance, and therefore with rhythm. Thus the rider should help his horse to establish a rhythm and should not rush or shorten up into a fence.

In the early stages of jump training, the horse should be fitted with a neck strap or a breast plate – which on occasion even the most experienced rider may need to hold (or the mane) if he is to avoid interfering with the horse's mouth.

The correct position for the rider is described in Chapter 1. It is usual with a young horse to adopt the forward seat, out of the saddle, in order to give the horse's back the freedom to work. However, the seat aids can be used momentarily with a horse who tries to stop, or who lacks impulsion. When working over trotting poles it is vital for the horse's back to be able to move freely and not to be made rigid or hollow. It is usual, therefore, to adopt rising trot; although sitting trot is acceptable for a rider with a good seat and a horse who is strong and supple in his back.

THE STAGES OF TRAINING

Trotting poles. Work over poles on the ground, at first singly and then in series, is an essential part of a young horse's general education. It is a useful gymnastic exercise which teaches him to lower his head and neck, to round his back, to flex his joints and also to co-ordinate the action of his limbs.

Distances between poles (Fig. 31). Whether on the ground or raised, these must accommodate the horse's stride exactly. For most horses and ponies, except very small ones, the optimum distances are 1 metre (3 ft) for the walking and 1.3-1.4 metres (4¼-4½ ft) for trotting. The latter is based on the trotting stride of the average horse. Unco-ordinated or big horses need 1.5 metres (5 ft); ponies may need 1.2 metres (4 ft). It is vital to maintain correct distances between poles on the ground. Slight adjustments should be made to suit the strides of different horses and the going (heavy going needs shorter; firm going needs longer). An assistant on the ground should be ready to re-position displaced poles or to adjust distances when they do not suit the stride of the horse.

Trotting poles   1.3-1.4 m

Trotting poles and fence   2.6-2.9 m

31. Diagram showing distances between trotting poles, and of a placing pole in front of a fence.

2.6-3 m

Placing pole and fence

TO RAISE THE POLES

These are best put on blocks which have been slightly hollowed out to enable the pole to be fitted and not to roll when hit. Light plastic blocks are ideal but cavaletti can be used as long as the ends are square and heavy. Those which have crossed ends are not advisable as the poles often roll when hit by a horse and can cause accidents. The practice of piling cavaletti on top of each other to form a jump is not recommended, for the same reason.

Technique. First walk the horse over a single pole. When he does this calmly, the number can be increased to two, three and then four. The poles can then be altered to trotting distances.

It is important for the horse to remain calm and to maintain a rhythm. If he gets excited, it sometimes helps to remove alternate poles. He can be trotted in a circle until he settles, and when he does so the poles can be tried again.

INTRODUCING OBSTACLES

When the horse trots over the poles correctly and calmly, a very small obstacle can be erected beyond the last trotting pole. It should look inviting, should not exceed 38 cm (1 ft 3 ins) in height, and preferably should consist of cross bars which direct the horse towards the centre of the fence. The aim is for the horse to land over the last pole and, without taking a stride, take off over the obstacle. The average horse needs between 2.6 metres (8 ft) and 2.9 metres (9½ ft) in front of the fence. Distances should be adjusted for long- or short-striding horses.

PLACING POLES

In order to help the horse arrive at a good position for take-off, especially in the early stages, when the rider should not interfere, it is advisable to use either trotting poles as above, or a single placing pole, which should be either 2.6 to 3 metres (8 to 10 ft) (no stride), or 5 to 6 metres (16½ to 20 ft) (one stride) in front of the jump.

TYPES OF OBSTACLE

As soon as the horse can jump a particular fence at the end of a line of trotting poles, or after a placing pole, calmly and in good style, he can be asked to jump a slightly higher, wider, or different type of obstacle in the same manner.

Single fences The horse must gradually be introduced to fences (which have groundlines) without trotting poles or a placing pole. The horse should learn to think for himself and should adjust his stride. If a horse starts to rush the fence, with inexperienced riders (and for the first few jumps in any lesson) reversion to use of a placing pole is of value.

117

Combinations The horse must gradually be introduced to series of fences between which he can take one or two strides. These should start very low so that the horse can gain his confidence.

A placing pole is usually introduced at the beginning of a series of fences between which he can take one or two strides. These should start very low so that the horse can gain confidence.

A placing pole is usually advisable in front of a small upright, then another fence at one stride (3.6 metres/18 ft) to a second fence at two strides (8.2 metres/27 ft).

As the horse becomes more confident and proficient, extra fences can be added and the heights and distances altered. The aim is to have the horse jumping in good style with a clear take-off platform. This means:

□ His front legs and hind legs should take off from almost the same place.
□ He should bend his front legs upwards, not backward, and they should remain a pair.
□ He should jump straight and not twist in the air.
□ He should jump calmly and in a good rhythm.

The distances between fences which suit most horses are in multiples of 2.7 metres (9 ft) to 3.3 metres (11 ft) with the fences not over 1 metre (3 ft). If the horse bends his front legs backwards, the distances are too short; if he flattens in outline between the fences, the distances are too long. The first fence should always be the smallest with the last fence the largest.

By altering the distances the horse can be taught to shorten and lengthen his stride and thus become more athletic. It is important to alter both heights and distances very gradually so that he does not lose confidence.

CANTERING

The non-jumping strides at the above distances are taken at the canter, but the approach should be at the trot. In the early stages of jump training it is advisable to approach all the fences at the trot as at this gait the horse is usually more balanced and the slower speed encourages him to bascule. Some riders allow their horses to break into the canter just before the obstacle, but it is not advisable to make the entire approach at the canter until the horse's work on the flat at this pace is satisfactory, and the fences are higher than about 1 metre (3 ft 3 ins). At the canter the horse takes in his stride tiny obstacles tending to flatten and failing to develop his bascule.

CHANGING THE DISTANCES

When the horse jumps combinations and grids with correct distances, calmly and in a fluent style, then the distances can be varied, but by inches only at a time, to teach him to jump from both long and short strides. It is best to keep any series of fences either for short strides or for long. Altering short and long distances is very difficult and is inadvisable for all except top horses and riders.

VARYING THE FENCES

The horse must be taught to jump all types of fences with confidence. He should be introduced to a miniature versions of all the fences found in the show ring – brightly coloured obstacles, walls, triple bars, oxers, planks, brushes, barrels, etc. When riding out, every opportunity can be taken to jump the young horse over strange obstacles, such as ditches, banks, hedges, logs, etc., as long as they are low enough not to over-face the pupil.

The water jump should also come into the training programme. Firstly, the horse must learn not to be frightened of it, so he can be walked through puddles and made to jump small streams and ditches, preferably following a more experienced horse. The first water jump he is asked to attempt should not be wide (a maximum of 3 metres [10 ft]). It is also advisable to put a pole of about .90 metres (3 ft) high over the centre of the water to encourage him to jump into the air, not just to pop over the brush into the water.

The rider should try to get the horse to approach the water with a little more speed than for a normal fence and to ask him to take off as close as possible to the water.

COURSES

A horse which is to compete must learn to jump series of fences other than in straight lines. Therefore, a short course of fences similar to, but less in number and smaller in height than, those in the show ring can be erected. The rider should try to give the horse the best possible approach to the fence so:

(a) He must not cut the corners but give the horse as many straight strides before the fence as possible.

(b) He must keep the horse balanced and in a rhythm. To do this he will probably need to half-halt and collect his horse immediately on landing over each fence and to make a great effort to turn each corner correctly.

(c) The horse must have enough impulsion (see page 77) to tackle the fences, but impulsion must not be confused with speed. Going fast will tend to make the horse flatten over the fences.

JUMPING AT SPEED

Most jump-offs are against the clock, so any horse and rider having had sufficient training to make winning a possibility must learn how to jump a course at speed. Galloping into the fences is rarely advisable with young horses, who tend to flatten and become careless. The horse must learn to

119

jump fences at angles and to be balanced enough to cut a corner and – having taken one or two strides – to jump the obstacle.

The rider should aim to maintain impulsion and rhythm when practising these techniques over small obstacles.

REFUSING

This is a problem which the trainer should try to avoid at all costs. Therefore never ask a horse to jump a fence at a height which he and his rider are not capable of negotiating. With strange obstacles, give the horse every opportunity to gain his confidence by starting very low, by having a more experienced horse jump first, and by making the fence as inviting as possible with a ground line, good width and wings to stop run-outs.

Should the horse refuse: if it is through lack of confidence or poor riding, lower the fence before trying again. If the horse is doing it out of mischief and is starting to do it frequently, he should be reprimanded once, and ridden strongly into fences.

If a horse that normally jumps well starts refusing, it is probable that he is in pain. Steps must be taken to discover the reason. It may be his feet, his back or his mouth that is hurting him.

RUSHING

Into the fence. This makes it difficult for the horse to be balanced and to arrive at the correct take-off position. It is often considered to be due to over-eagerness: but, on the contrary, it is usually due to lack of confidence and the horse trying to get the frightening operation (of jumping) over as quickly as possible.

TO CORRECT:

□ The rider must give the horse confidence, which is best done by jumping frequently over small single fences, so that it becomes part of the routine rather than a major operation. Consecutive fences should not be attempted. After jumping a fence, settle the horse before attempting another.

□ The rider can circle his horse in front of the fence until he settles into a rhythm, and only then allow him to jump.

□ Trotting poles can be placed in front of the obstacle. It is usually best to walk into the first pole of the line.

□ Small grids can be used frequently.

□ Jump on a circle with a short approach.

After the fence. It is important for the horse to be balanced as soon as possible after the fence and not to rush off. If the voice and half-halts (but not pulling on the reins) are not effective then place a pole at either 6.5 metres (21 ft) or 9.5 metres (31 ft) after the fence.

120

TAKING OFF TOO CLOSE

Horses which take off too close to a fence lack scope and/or confidence.
TO CORRECT:
□ The horse must be given sufficient impulsion to clear the fence.
□ A take-off rail should be placed about a foot out from the base of each fence.
□ The distances between combination fences can be gradually lengthened so that he learns to extend his stride and to take off further away.
□ Use placing poles to get the horse to stand back.

JUMPING WITH A HOLLOW BACK

Horses tend to jump with a flat or hollow back if they approach the fences too fast and/or take off far away.
TO CORRECT:
□ Jump fences out of a trot rather than a canter.
□ Use placing poles in front of the fences to encourage him to get underneath the fences. Begin with a distance which is easy for him, and gradually shorten it so that he has to take off closer to the fence.
□ Jump plenty of low, wide parallels which encourage a horse to bascule and to fold his forelegs.
□ Use plenty of grids with relatively short distances between the fences.

FAMILIARISATION

A horse's first show is usually a nerve-racking experience. It is therefore advisable to take him to a show before he starts competing and to get him relaxed in this stimulating atmosphere.

11 Cross-country Training

INTRODUCTION

To be successful across country the horse must be able to cope with the great range of problems found in today's competitions. Both horse and rider must learn through careful thorough training and familiarisation how to approach and jump the variety of fences met in horse trials.

EARLY TRAINING

The aims of early training are to teach the horse:
- To regulate pace and cope with slopes and all types of going, including entering water.
- To respect solid fences.
- To become a safe conveyance across country by being encouraged from the beginning to work things out for himself.
- To be tough and able to perform in all types of weather. He should not be over 'cosseted'.

Flat work. This should continue in the manner described in Chapter 8.

Jumping exercises. The horse's athletic ability is built up over a period of months by varying the exercises over trotting poles, grids and small fences, jumped at angles from both trot and canter. At these angled fences the rider must be able to use each hand independently to effectively guide the horse and keep the legs against the horse's sides at all times.

Jumping exercises should be carried out up to two to three times a week in between flat work and hacks, and these should be based on the work discussed in the previous chapter.

Hacking. Whilst out hacking the horse should learn to cope with all types of going and terrain. He has to be able to balance himself when riding up and down hills and over rough ground. It is best to use a loose rein as much as possible so that he can think and hold himself without reliance on the rider. Popping over little fences, such as logs and ditches, when out hacking will teach him to be alert and quick-thinking. Water should be ridden through and over whenever possible.

It is vital that the horse is never frightened, so:

☐ Everything attempted should be within the horse's capabilities for his stage of training.

☐ The fence should be safe, with good take-offs and landings. A nasty experience in the early stages could undermine a horse's confidence.

Schooling over cross-country fences. This can begin once the horse is (a) confident when jumping fences on flat ground or just over 1 metre (3 ft 6 ins), (b) balanced and controllable enough to jump combinations and (c) able to lengthen and shorten his stride. Several sessions may be required. The first should be over straightforward fences of different types up to 0.90 metre (3 ft). In succeeding sessions, start with a few simple obstacles and gradually increase the questions asked by including ditches and rails, steps, banks, bullfinches, rails at varying angles, and corners. The horse should be progressively familiarised with the types of fence which are met with on cross-country courses. Always finish on a good note – before the horse becomes too tired.

Hunting. Some horses learn the techniques of cross-country jumping much more quickly than others, but they all benefit from a season's hunting, which teaches both rider and horse to go boldly across country and to think quickly over unfamiliar ground. This is how horses learn to produce a 'fifth leg' and become adept at jumping the unexpected.

Hunter trials. Once the horse jumps small cross-country fences confidently, he can be entered in novice hunter trials. Pair classes may benefit the timid horse if a more experienced horse is the pair and leads to give him confidence.

Progression to more advanced competitions depends on how the horse tackles the small ones. As long as he goes well at the lower level, he can be asked a bit more and the difficulty can be increased as and when the horse is confident enough to cope. Never ever ask too much at once.

TYPES OF FENCE

Cross-country fences can be divided into several categories according to the method of riding needed to negotiate them safely at the faster speed used when cross-country riding.

Respect is needed for every fence. Each type of fence must be treated with respect. All too often it is the 'simple' ones which cause the most trouble. This is usually because most thought goes into approaching and riding the more difficult fences – so that they often cause comparatively few problems. The rider must treat each fence as if it is *the* most important one, so that the horse is given the maximum help throughout. Ridden in this way, horses build up confidence in their rider and vice versa, and the combination then becomes a partnership, each confident in their ability to jump any course attempted. Confidence is one of the most important aspects of cross-country riding.

Upright fences

Uprights should present few problems, although the degree of difficulty will depend on how and where they are built. The rider must check:

☐ To see if there is a false ground line (the pole on or nearest to the ground is behind the higher poles). Horse and rider usually judge the take-off point by looking at this lowest pole. If they do so when it is a false groundline they will get too close to the fence.

☐ If the ground is uneven.

☐ Whether the fence can be easily seen from the line of approach.

☐ The height of the fence.

AIMS

☐ To ride straight at the fence in almost all cases.

☐ To be accurate, never asking for too much of a stand-off, nor getting too close.

☐ To build up plenty of impulsion if the upright is sited on the top of a hill. This will ensure that the horse's hocks are underneath him before he takes off.

☐ If at the bottom of a hill, uprights must be approached at a steady pace, making sure that the horse is not on his forehand but well between the hand and leg. Then he can take off easily yet remain balanced on landing.

Spread fences

AIMS

☐ To ride with plenty of impulsion. Approaching too slowly will necessitate last minute effort, which could easily frighten a young horse.

☐ To take care not to let the horse stand off too far and so make the fence unnecessarily wide.

☐ If the spreads are sloped, the rider should not ask for too big a stand-off and should allow the horse as much rein as he needs.

☐ If they are parallels they should be ridden-at straight and accurately, keeping the horse well between hand and leg, and not on the forehand. If he is to avoid disastrous results he must get off the ground in time to clear the front rail.

Ditches and open water

☐ Ditches must be ridden at strongly, particularly on the 'spooky' type of horse who may tend to have a last-minute look.

☐ Open water must be ridden at strongly, but accurately, encouraging the horse to spring up into the air. Strong legs are applied and a good contact on the reins maintained to keep him up so that he jumps the obstacles clearly. Often the edges to ditches and open water are a bit soft.

32. *A trakehner.*

33. *A tiger trap.*

□ Large, wide ditches or 'graves' need very strong riding with legs and sometimes with the seat and a good firm contact on the reins, to encourage the horse to go upwards and forwards. When ridden this way they rarely cause trouble despite their horrific appearance.

□ Open ditches with brush and with rails must always be boldly ridden.

□ Rails over ditches, trakehners and tiger traps (Figs 32 and 33) often cause trouble because the horse (and rider) tend to look down into them and then lose the impulsion to clear the fence. Firm riding with plenty of leg, encouraging the horse forward and upward, is needed at this type of fence which, although simple, often causes problems on novice courses.

□ Angled rails over a ditch are generally best approached straight and in the middle, or slightly to the side, where the rail is farthest away, as the ditch can help by acting as a nice ground-line.

Water

Water must be ridden into with a great deal of thought and care.

ASSESSING THE WATER

It is difficult to judge the pace at which any fence into water is best jumped unless the depth and landing are known. Therefore, before attempting it on horseback, it is advisable to walk through the water to ensure that the base

125

is even and does not have any holes or soft patches, to measure the depth, and to find out whether the water is fast flowing or still.

AIMS WHEN RIDING

☐ The approach should not be too fast, as the drag of the water on landing tends to tip the horse on to his forehand. Coming in too slowly, however, can cause an unnecessary stop. A good strong trot or 'bouncy canter' is usually the best pace.

☐ The horse should be encouraged to jump out as far as possible so that he does not land too steeply.

☐ As most water jumps involve some degree of drop, the rider adjusts his position to prevent being thrown forward on landing. This helps the horse keep his balance and enables him to be ridden forward immediately.

☐ Fences in water or which have water in front of them are best approached at a trot to avoid sending up too much spray, which can unsight the horse.

Many falls would be prevented if water were ridden at a sensible pace. A definite, controlled approach and control on landing are the two vital factors.

Combinations

All combinations require accurate and controlled riding and the more difficult ones really test the athletic ability of a horse.

AIMS WHEN RIDING

● *Rails at varying angles to each other.* These need practice at home so that the horse is familiar with all the differing forms of one and two stride distances (page 118). The line of approach is of the utmost importance. Once the best line has been determined, a straight route through the obstacle is the secret of success. Having decided on the route which will give the horse the best distances, it is vital to arrive at the exact spot for take-off. Therefore a line through the obstacle is determined by going from one specific landmark straight towards another: e.g. from a conveniently situated tree to a certain telegraph pole.

● *Bounces,* which demand great agility, are very difficult for stiff horses. They must be approached steadily, but with plenty of impulsion so that the horse resembles a tightly coiled spring being released over each jump. Approaching this type of obstacle too fast with the horse on the forehand is inviting disaster. Controlled forward impulsion should be aimed at. Grid work is the introduction to this, but practice over higher fences with wider distances is necessary to teach the horse to use himself correctly. Start with very small fences with the distance between 3 metres (10 ft) and 3.3 metres (11 ft). As the height is increased the distance can be lengthened to 3.6 metres (12 ft) or more to suit the strides of the horse.

Bounces demand great effort from the horse and should not be overdone. Two or three successful attempts are sufficient. The horse should always be well loosened up before practising this type of exercise.

126

34. A coffin. The rails in front of the ditch should be fixed, so that if hit by a horse he does not carry them down the bank with him, which could cause a fall.

Coffins (Fig. 34)
These are fences which catch out the unwary and should be mastered before tackling them in competition.

TO PRACTISE
Once the horse is confident when jumping all types of ditches he can be introduced to rails one or two strides immediately after a ditch and then progress to jumping rails in front of the ditch. As soon as he is confident he can be asked to jump rails – ditch – rails, varying the distances of the rails on either side of the ditch.

AIMS WHEN RIDING
□ The approach is all important, but the technique depends on the siting of the fence. The usual siting is downhill to the first section with the last element uphill. Coffins require steady but determined riding. The horse may not see the ditch until the last moment, so the important factor is for him to have sufficient impulsion and to be ridden forward in the last few strides, which will make it difficult for him to stop.
□ As the 'out' of the coffin is often uphill and can be rather close to the ditch, the horse must be kept in balance and not allowed to 'launch off' from the bottom and then fail to clear the final element.
□ The position of the rider at such fences is particularly important. If he gets too far in front or behind the movement of the horse at the crucial moment he may hinder the horse and prevent him from completing the fence.

Banks
AIMS WHEN RIDING
□ Banks must be ridden at with great impulsion, but not too fast, as when jumping uphill a horse loses momentum. This is an important principle of cross-country riding. Momentum is gained when jumping downhill, and is lost uphill. Allowance must be made for this.
□ They should be approached straight.
□ Once on top of a bank the rider must maintain forward impulsion.
□ On landing, balance the horse by maintaining an upright position and not allowing the legs to move backwards.
□ With a Normandy bank – a bank with rails off – maintain plenty of

forward impulsion, especially at those fences designed for an on-off jump. The horse should be allowed to jump out well to avoid a 'peck' landing, which may follow if this type of jump is ridden at too slowly.

Steps and drops

AIMS WHEN RIDING

☐ Steps up require enough impulsion to overcome the shortening effect of jumping uphill. If there are several, the 'push' must be maintained to the top.

☐ Drop fences or steps down require the horse to be steadied so that he does not land with too much impetus which he will then be unable to control. The rider should keep the weight upright and off the forehand. Steps down are best approached from trot.

Corners

Corners require an accurate, calculated approach and an ability to ride straight. It is safest to choose the line as shown in Fig. 35.

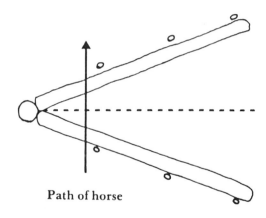

35. A corner fence showing the safest path for the horse: i.e. at right angles to a line which bisects the corner.

Path of horse

ASSESSING CORNERS

The line of approach must be determined, allowing enough room to jump: not so close to the apex and the flag that there is danger of running out, yet not too far in, where the fence becomes too wide to jump safely. Study the fence carefully on foot, so that the spot to be jumped is clear. Then move back from the fence to see the line that you wish to approach. Choose a suitable landmark which will not be obscured when riding – that is, on the far side – and aim to ride at it to ensure that the fence is met absolutely right.

AIMS WHEN RIDING

Ride to the landmarks. Take the fence with precision. This will ensure a good ride over a corner fence.

128

JUMPING AT SPEED

Cross-country jumping requires a faster speed than show jumping. The rider should help the horse to negotiate the solid, fixed obstacles by riding sensibly and keeping the horse under control at all times. As the horse gains experience the speed can be increased, but the horse must always be listening and obedient so that he can be balanced for the turns and fences. A good steady rhythm, avoiding unnecessary pulling, and aiming always for the most direct route from one fence to another, are more important than speed and will take less out of the horse.

THE RIDER'S POSITION

He should be in the galloping position with shortened leathers, the seat out of the saddle, and a good contact on the reins. On approaching a fence the horse should be steadied and balanced with the legs. The rider should lower his seat to the degree necessary to maintain the impulsion needed by a particular fence: e.g. steadier at uprights than those with a good ground line. Upon landing, the galloping position should then be resumed.

GALLOPING

The gallop must be perfected before entering more advanced events. This will also help to clear the horse's wind and make him fit. When out hacking, the horse should learn to canter on strongly, remaining obedient and calm. It should be remembered that flat-out galloping is not required on cross-country courses, and when preparing for one-day events it is important to practise cantering at a strong pace up and down hills and over fences. For two- and three-day events the horse should learn to gallop, but it is a mistake to over-gallop him as this will wear him out or lame him before getting to the competition.

Galloping should always be on the best possible ground and, if possible, slightly uphill, as this puts far less strain on the horse's legs while still helping to clear his wind.

Galloping should not be attempted until the horse is fit and has been in serious work for at least six to eight weeks. Start with a five- or six-furlong gallop, being careful to keep the horse balanced and well between hand and leg. Begin fairly slowly and then push the horse on for the last quarter mile, to make him blow. Bring him back steadily to a walk. Never allow him to flounder along. Loosen the girths and walk until he has cooled off and stopped blowing.

The amount of galloping and distance will depend on each horse and on the terrain, as galloping uphill makes the horse work harder than on the flat.

INTERVAL TRAINING

This is an alternative to galloping as a means of getting a mature eventer fit. Several short periods of work are alternated with brief recovery periods (the intervals). It is based on methods devised by Jack le Goff and adapted from interval training methods used by athletes.

Principles
□ The body will adapt itself to the stress of demands made upon it, as long as it is given time. Therefore repeatedly small but increased demands are made upon it.
□ The intervals are timed so that the recovery is not quite achieved before the next period of work.
□ The work periods are designed to avoid maximum stress, so that the respiratory, cardio-vascular and muscular systems are all gradually developed.
□ It is used not more than once every three or four days as it takes this long for the metabolism to return to normal.

Use. Interval training is only suitable for
□ A mature horse.
□ A sound horse.
□ A horse who has completed 4 to 8 weeks of basic fittening and conditioning work (i.e. capable of hacking for two hours).

Timing. 6 to 12 weeks of interval training are needed before a three-day event.

The programme. A programme is devised so that the distance and speeds are gradually increased. It is geared to at least two competitions.

Before cantering, the horse should be warmed-up with 30 minutes of walking and trotting.

After cantering he should be cooled down by gentle work for up to an hour. This is essential to help the vascular system remove waste products accumulated during exercise.

All work must be carried out with the horse going into the bridle and on the aids.

An individual programme
It is vital for the programme to be adjusted to suit the needs of the individual horse. The aspects which can be varied are:
● *The intervals.* Range of one to four minutes. Four minutes may be needed for the horse to 'almost' recover at the beginning of training, but only one minute if the horse is very fit.
● *Work periods*
□ *Duration.* Range 3 to 12 minutes, but in total a training session should

not be more than 35 minutes. The aim is to work up to cantering at least the distance of the steeplechase and cross-country combined.

N.B. Excitable horses can be cantered for longer distances more slowly.

□ *Number*. A maximum of three work periods.

□ *Frequency*. Interval training may be used once to twice a week. With a young horse, once a week might be sufficient, but it is usual to progress to twice a week.

□ *Speeds*. These range from trot, to a canter at about 600 metres per minute. Young horses might begin their interval training with trot periods, but the major part of the work is done at 'half speed' – a canter of approximately 400m./min. As the horse becomes fitter it can be increased to 500m./min. and eventually for ½ mile or 1 mile periods at 600 m./min.

N.B. Horses competing in one- or two-day events before the three-day event need not do faster work until the last two or three weeks. Horses with bad legs should work up hills instead of the faster work, and depending on their 'wind' may need one or two pipe-openers, going at close to maximum speed for 500m. uphill 10 days before the event.

□ *Terrain*. If hilly, distances can be reduced by up to 25 per cent.

N.B. Varied terrain helps to keep the horse fresh.

• *Work on non-cantering days*. If the horse works strongly for 1½ hours on these days, less cantering may be needed. If he does not do much, more may be needed. Work on non-cantering days depends on the particular trainer and is a major cause of differences in cantering programmes.

N.B. After a competition a horse will need usually a minimum of seven days before cantering again.

• *The horse*. The type of horse and how recently he has been fit affects the programme. A small Thoroughbred which has been very fit in the near past needs less work than a cold-blooded horse which has never been really fit.

Evaluating fitness

• *Heart and respiration rates*. Heart rates can vary, but once a norm has been established a record of the levels and recovery rates of the heart and respiration help in the evaluation of fitness. For an accurate comparison the same amount of exercise and the same intervals after work must be taken. One method is to compare rates every 10 days by cantering up the same hill, stopping, and taking the rates after one, five and ten minutes. As training progresses, the rates should drop.

The pulse at rest is normally between 36 to 44 beats per minute and top rate is over 200. For maximum training effect the pulse rate should stay between 80 and 150 while the horse is working.

Respiration at rest is normally 10 to 16 and it should not go above 100 during work.

'False' readings can occur, as an excited horse has a high pulse and a hot horse can respire very quickly. Establish a normal pattern for each individual horse in a given situation.

• *Feel*. It is the experienced eye of the trainer and the feel of the rider which judge the fitness of the horse and his best programme of work. There is no substitute for knowing one's horse, for he is a unique living animal with his own capabilities, limitations and requirements.

THE START AND FINISH

The start. This is important, as a quick getaway can save valuable seconds. Practise walking into a start box or similar area.

Keeping quite calm, walk in a small circle until the starter begins the count-down at five seconds. Walk into the box and face away from the exit. Quietly turn round so that the horse is ready and does not get upset. The rider should not fight the exuberant horse. He will settle far more quickly if the rider sits quite still and keeps a firm contact on the reins.

The finish. After passing the finish keep hold of the horse's head and bring him gradually back to a walk. Flopping in on a loose rein at speed is foolish, as tired horses easily break down if they stumble.

CARRYING WEIGHTS

This rarely causes trouble as long as the weight is evenly spread on either side, in a weight cloth. Always remember to pull the weight cloth up under the front of the saddle before tightening the girths. It can be uncomfortable if allowed to press down on the withers. It is a good idea to practise riding with weights if the horse has not had them on before, and if a large amount has to be carried a few jumping sessions will accustom the horse to the difference.

SAFETY EQUIPMENT

Safety when jumping a cross-country cannot be too strongly stressed. Over-reach boots, brushing boots, surcingle and a breast plate are strongly advised. Studs should be used behind, and in front if the going is slippery. Crash hats are compulsory in horse trials and cross-country events. Back protectors are strongly recommended.

SUMMARY

The need for patience and thoughtful training cannot be over-stressed: they are vital in the education of a young horse. If time is spent in the beginning gradually increasing the ability and confidence of the horse, the outcome should be rewarded by many happy hours riding across country in what is a thrilling and most exciting aspect of equestrian sport.

Conversion Table

1600 m = 1 mile approx.   ½ speed = 400 m/m approx.

2400 m = 1½ miles approx.   ¾ speed = 600 m/m approx.

3200 m = 2 miles approx.   max speed = 800 m/m approx.

A possible programme of interval training to prepare a horse for a three-day event

THE BASIC CONDITIONING WORK HAVING BEEN COMPLETED

N.B. *Where speeds are not stated, simply divide distance by number of minutes:*
i.e. Week 1 4/1600 m is 400 m/m.

Week	Session	Minutes/ distance of 1st work period	Minutes of rest	Minutes/ distance of 2nd work period	Minutes of rest	Minutes/ distance of 3rd work period
1	a	4/1600 m				
	b	6/2400 m				
2		4/1600 m	3	4/1600 m		
3	a	4/1600 m	3	6/2400 m		
	b	4/1600 m	3	6/2400 m		
	c	6/2400 m	3	6/2400 m		
4	a	6/2400 m	3	6/2400 m	3	6/2400 m
	b	4/1600 m	3	6/2400 m		
5	a	6/2400 m	3	8/3200 to build up to 520 m/m for last 500m.		
	b	6/2400 m	3	8/3200 m 520 m/m for 500 m plus 600 m/m for last 500 m.		
6		One-day Event 3800 m at 520 m/m cross-country. Rest.*				

7	a	5/2000 m	3	7/2800 m 500m/m for last 800 m.		
	b	6/3400 m	2	9/2600 m 600 m/m.		
8	a	6/2400 m	3	6/2400 m 520 m/m.	2	8/3200 m starting at 500 m/m build-up to 650 m/m for last 1600 m.
	b	9/3600 m 570 m/m for 500 m	2	8/3200 m starting 550 m/m 700 m/m		
9		Two-day Event Steeplechase 3000 m at 690 m/m – Cross-country 5500 m at 570 m/m Rest.*				
10	a	6/2400 m	3	8/3200 m 550 m for last 500 m.		
	b	7/2800 m	2	9/3600 m 650 m.		
11	a	9/600 m 550 m/m for 800 m.	2	8/3200 m starting 550 m/m building up to 700 m/m for last 1600 m.		
	b	6/2400 m	2	6/2400 m starting 500 m/m building up to 600 m/m		
12		Pipe-opener day before Endurance Test 500 m uphill at 750 m/m.	1	4/1600 m at 700 m/m.		

*More rest days may be necessary according to the individual horse.

Index

Aids 24, 25, 27, 73, 75-6, 78, 84-5,
  87-8, 97-8, 102, 105, 110;
  artificial 29, 35; driving 77, 87;
  lateral 30, 88; lungeing 60;
  natural 29-35; 'on the aids' 84,
  96; theory 29-36; use of 37-46;
  weight aids 31
Amble 50

Backing 63, 66-7, 70-2, 114
Balance: rider's 11, 17, 19-20, 23-4,
  25; horse's 24, 52, 57, 60, 62-3,
  77, 78, 81-2, 84-6, 88-9, 96-7,
  100, 105-6, 115, 122
Banks 127-8
Basculing 79, 112, 118, 121
Bit 21, 32, 57-8, 62, 67-9, 72; above
  the bit, 63, 82; accepts the bit 32,
  63, 77, 81-3, 84-5, 87, 88, 100,
  103; behind the bit, 63, 83; on
  the bit 50, 53-5, 81, 94-6, 100,
  106, 108, 110; bit rein 33-4
Boots 21, 58, 61, 67, 70, 114;
  brushing 22, 76, 132; over-reach
  132
Bounces 126
Breast plate 58, 67, 68, 71, 72, 115,
  132
Bridle 61, 67-8, 70; double 33-4,
  100; snaffle 21, 33, 57, 67, 71,
  76, 108
Bridoon 33-4

Cadence 45, 52, 78, 84, 97, 106-7,
  110

Canter 38, 51-2, 53-6, 73, 74, 78-9,
  86, 88-91, 95-6, 99, 103-4, 106-7,
  122, 129; counter-canter 44,
  90-1, 95, 96-7, 104, 107;
  disunited 51-2; jumping 118,
  121; lungeing horse 60-1, 63, 65;
  lungeing rider 25-6; rider's
  position 16-17; strike-off (See
  transitions.)
Cavaletti 116-17
Cavesson: lunge cavesson, 21, 57-8,
  61, 62, 67-71, 108, 114; cavesson
  noseband (See noseband.)
Change of leg 44; flying change
  44-5, 90, 95, 96-7, 101, 104,
  105-6; simple change 44, 90-1,
  95-6, 104
Circles 13, 22, 39-40, 57, 59-61,
  63-5, 70, 72, 79, 85-6, 90-1, 95,
  97-8, 100, 103-4, 107
Coffin 127
Collection 39, 52-3, 70, 81, 83-5,
  89-90, 91, 95-9, 102-10; collected
  gaits 38, 54, 55-6, 65, 103-5
Combinations 118, 123, 126
Corners 128
Counter change of hand 104-5
Cross-country training 122-35

Diagonals, changing the 24, 96
Distances 64, 88, 113-15, 116-19,
  121, 126
Ditches 119, 124-5, 127
Dressage 101-2; competitions 111;
  rules for 37; tests 46, 90
Drops 128

Events: one-day 90, 129, 131, 134;
    two-day 129, 131, 135; three-day
    101, 129, 131, 134-5
Exercises: horse 79-80, 82, 95, 99;
    jumping 85, 88, 90, 116, 121;
    rider 23, 25-8
Extension 38, 52-4, 65, 81, 102-4,
    110; extended gaits 38, 54-5, 91

Facilities 21-2, 76, 102
Feeding 67, 103
F.E.I. (Fédération Equestre
    Internationale) 11, 37, 101
Figures 85-6, 91, 92-3, 98
Fitness 27-8, 57, 60, 129-30, 131-2
Flying change (*See* change of leg.)
Foal 66, 68
Forgeing 48
Free gaits 32-3, 52, 56, 61

Gaits 16, 23, 49-56, 70, 77-8, 84,
    85-6, 89-90, 97-8, 103; lungeing
    60, 63
Gallop 52, 89; training 129
Goff, Jack le 130
Grand Prix 91
Grids 118, 120-1, 126

Hacking 46, 89, 122-3, 129-30
Half-halt 38, 39, 42-3, 44-5, 79, 87,
    90, 106, 120-1
Half-pass 41, 43, 44, 90, 93, 97,
    99-100, 104-5, 107
Halt 39, 61, 71-3, 86, 87-8, 90-1, 94,
    95, 104, 108, 110
Handler, Hans 77, 102
Hands 27, 36, 82-3, 87; aids 31-4,
    38-9, 78, 81-2, 86-7, 94-5, 108,
    122; inside/outside 32; position
    12-13, 16-17, 19, 22, 26
Hips 4, 15, 19, 27, 31; bones
    14-15, 24; collapsed 12, 13, 15;
    joints 11, 12, 14-17, 19, 23, 26, 38
Horsemastership 76, 103
Hunter Trials 123

Hunting 123

Impulsion 31-2, 35, 38-9, 42-3, 45,
    51-5, 65, 77, 81, 83-4, 86-7,
    89-90, 94, 95-8, 100, 102-6,
    108-11, 113, 115-6, 119-21, 123-9
Inside 37; inside hand 32; inside leg
    30, 39-44; inside rein 40-3, 63,
    70, 82
Instructor when lungeing 22
Interval training 130-2, 134-5

Jumping 79; jumping at speed
    119-20, 129; lungeing 64-5,
    113-15; rider's position 17-19;
    training the horse 112-21; whip
    34-5

Lateral work 32, 40, 41-4, 70, 79,
    88, 90, 93, 97, 98, 100, 104-5
Leading in hand 68-9, 71-3
Leathers 19, 71; length of leathers
    24
Leg yield 40, 42, 90, 93, 97-8, 100
Legs 25, 27; aids 30, 32-3, 35,
    37-45, 73, 77-8, 79-84, 87-8, 94,
    99, 105-6, 111, 115; inside/
    outside leg 17, 30, 79; leading leg
    38, 44-5, 51-2, 95-6; leg position
    12, 14, 17-19, 23, 25, 27, 122
Loins 15-16, 23, 25
Long reining 70
Loose schooling 113-14
Lungeing: dress for 21;
    horse 57-65, 66-7, 69, 70-2, 111,
    113, 114; rider 20-8

Martingales 29
Medium gaits 38, 52-3, 54, 63, 65,
    91, 104
Mounting 71-2, 73-4
Movements 91-3; aids for 37-46;
    basic training 87-8; lateral 90;
    intermediate training 90-101;
    advanced training 102-11

Neck strap 67, 72, 115
Noseband 21; cavesson 21, 57-8, 76; dropped 21, 57-8, 76; flash 76

Outside 37; outside hand 32; outside leg 30, 40-44; outside rein 39-43, 63, 70, 82
Overtracking 54-5

Pace 50
Passade 106-7
Passage 45, 65, 104, 110-11
Pelvis 12, 14-17, 31
Piaffe 44, 45, 65, 104, 107-10, 111
Pirouette 41, 43, 46, 93; canter pirouette 106-7; walk pirouette 100, 106, 110
Poles 64; placing 114, 116, 117, 118, 120-1; trotting 113, 116, 117, 120
Position 11-19, 20-8; basic 11, 19-20, 22-3, 76; classical 11; lungeing 59; jumping 5, 11, 17-19, 73, 127, 129; right and left 38, 40, 44-5

Quarters in/out 43, 99

Refusing 114-15, 120
Rein 13, 16-17, 19-20, 25-6, 32-4, 72, 77, 84, 87; bit/curb rein 33; contact 16, 18, 19, 32-3, 37, 39, 40, 45, 63, 80-3, 87-8, 95, 99, 115; draw rein 29; holding the reins 33-4; lead rein 68-9; long rein 33, 75, 85; loose 32-3, 122, 132; lungeing 21-2, 57-64, 67, 70-4, 108-9; outside/ inside rein (see outside/inside); running 29; side 21-3, 58, 61-4, 67, 73, 108; snaffle 34
Rein-back 39, 46, 90, 94-5, 104
Renvers 41, 43, 93, 99, 104, 105
Rewards 61, 72, 75-6, 95, 114
Rhythm 25-6, 45, 49-53, 55, 63-5, 77, 78, 79, 81, 84-6, 89, 94-8, 103-6, 115, 117, 119-20, 129
Riding out 88-9, 90, 112

Roller 58, 61-2, 67-8, 70
Rushing 64, 114, 120

Saddle 16-17, 22, 25-7, 58, 62-3, 67-8, 71-2, 107-8, 110
Safety equipment 132
Seat 11-19, 23-6, 38, 78, 84, 86-7, 94, 107, 115; aids 31, 38-9, 77, 80, 83, 87, 116; balance 17, 19; bones 11, 14-19, 23, 27, 31, 38, 45, 72, 86; collapsed 12; driving 111; hollow 12
Serpentine 86, 90, 91, 92, 95, 97, 104
Shoulder-in 40, 42, 46, 79-80, 90, 93, 98-9, 100, 105, 107, 109
Show jumping 90, 101
Shying 46, 74
Simple change (See change of leg.)
Spanish Riding School 11
Spread fences 124
Spurs 29-30, 35, 58
Start (cross country) 132
Steps and drops 128
Straightness 52, 63, 77, 80-1, 84-5, 89-90, 96-7, 98, 103, 105, 109, 127-8
Strides: even 50, 52-3; regular 53-5, 109
Strike off (See transitions, upward.)
Studs 132
Submission 77, 81-2, 83-4, 89, 103
Suppleness 28, 52, 65, 77, 78-9, 84, 88-9, 91, 95, 97-9, 112
Surcingle 132

Tack 21-2, 57-8, 67-8, 70-2, 76; lungeing 17, 57-8
Tempo 78, 111
Tone 11-12, 24
Traffic 74
Transitions 25-6, 44, 79, 85-6, 91, 94, 104, 108, 110; downward 38-9, 82, 86, 90, 104; upward (including strike-offs) 37-8, 86, 90, 96, 104, 106-7, 109

Index

Travers 41, 42, 43, 99, 100, 104, 107
Trot 12, 16, 29, 44-5, 49, 50, 51-6,
    72-4, 78-9, 82, 84-6, 88, 91, 98-9,
    103-5, 108-11, 113-14, 116-18,
    121-2, 130-1; lungeing rider
    24-6; lungeing horse 61, 63-5;
    rider's position 16
Turn on the forehand 40, 41, 46, 87,
    88, 93

Upright fences 124, 129

Voice aids 29, 60-1, 69, 73, 77, 86-7,
    108, 114, 120
Volte 100, 107
von Blixen-Finecke 39

Walk 44, 49-50, 52-6, 72-4, 78-9,
    82, 85-6, 88, 95-6, 98-100, 103-4,
    108, 110-11, 113; lungeing rider
    23-7, lungeing horse 61-4; rider's
    position 16
Water 119, 122, 124, 125-6
Weights 132
Whip 29, 69, 108-11; aids 35, 60,
    77, 114-5; changing hands 35;
    lunge whip 20, 22, 58-61, 67, 70,
    114; jumping 35; schooling 35,
    74, 76
Working gaits 38, 52, 53, 54, 63, 86

Xenophon 11

Yoga 28